T0318255

Entrepreneurial Urban Regeneration

In today's world, towns and cities dynamically develop over time and that's why urban regeneration is a widely experienced phenomenon. How can Business Improvement Districts (BIDs) create necessary conditions for the development of these phenomena? What is the role that BIDs have in entrepreneurial urbanism, supporting SMEs, city marketing and city branding? These are questions examined in this volume, in an effort to provide an extensive analysis of business improvement districts.

Enriched with an analysis of various case studies, including South Africa, Ontario, Tokyo, Barcelona, Slovenia and with an in-field analysis of a cultural heritage site, Korca, Albania, the book analyzes the importance, benefits, and impacts of this kind of organization. It highlights the social, economic, and ecologic challenges to the historic city markets today, which led to their rapid stagnancy. This book offers a practical and structured guide of the concept of Business Improvement Districts and highlights the best practices for management, financing, and organizing. It sheds light on the impacts and benefits of business improvement districts, offering conclusions about their influence on the future improvement of cultural and urban sites.

It will be of value to researchers, academics, professionals, and students in the fields of management, organizational studies, strategy, and sustainable development of tourism districts.

Rezart Prifti is a Lecturer and Researcher at Tirana University, Faculty of Economy, Tirana, Albania.

Fatma Jaupi is a Lecturer and Researcher at Tirana University, Faculty of Economy, Tirana, Albania.

Routledge Focus on Business and Management

The fields of business and management have grown exponentially as areas of research and education. This growth presents challenges for readers trying to keep up with the latest important insights. Routledge Focus on Business and Management presents small books on big topics and how they intersect with the world of business research.

Individually, each title in the series provides coverage of a key academic topic, whilst collectively, the series forms a comprehensive collection across the business disciplines.

The Customer Experience Model
Adyl Aliekperov

Organizational Justice and Organizational Change
Managing By Love
Dominique A. David

Cultural Proximity and Organization
Managing Diversity and Innovation
Federica Ceci and Francesca Masciarelli

Entrepreneurial Urban Regeneration
Business Improvement Districts as a Form
of Organizational Innovation
Rezart Prifti and Fatma Jaupi

For more information about this series, please visit: www.routledge.com/ Routledge-Focus-on-Business-and-Management/book-series/FBM

Entrepreneurial Urban Regeneration

Business Improvement Districts as a
Form of Organizational Innovation

**Rezart Prifti and
Fatma Jaupi**

Routledge
Taylor & Francis Group

NEW YORK AND LONDON

First published 2021
by Routledge
605 Third Avenue, New York, NY 10017

and by Routledge
2 Park Square, Milton Park, Abingdon, Oxon, OX14 4RN

First issued in paperback 2022

Routledge is an imprint of the Taylor & Francis Group, an informa business

© 2021 Taylor & Francis

Publisher's Note
The publisher has gone to great lengths to ensure the quality of
this reprint but points out that some imperfections in the original
copies may be apparent.

Library of Congress Cataloging-in-Publication Data
A catalog record for this title has been requested

ISBN 13: 978-0-367-61071-5 (pbk)
ISBN 13: 978-0-367-61068-5 (hbk)
ISBN 13: 978-1-003-10312-7 (ebk)

DOI: 10.4324/9781003103127

Typeset in Times New Roman
by codeMantra

Contents

1 The Multi-Facet Nature of Innovation

Innovation is omnipresent. It certainly is so in the world of technology and production, but also in other disciplines, such as social processes, arts, and management, albeit not as frequently discussed. Modern economic settings and business models have come to capitalize on innovation like no other force has. Innovation is intrinsic to business growth to such a degree that authors (e.g., Godin, 2008) have stated that most people instinctively equate innovation with technological innovation. Innovation has become a quintessential concept to our society that Nowotny (2006) has defined our epoch as one of "a quest for innovation". But, what particularly defines innovation, and how did it evolve to this point?

Innovation, as we view it today, became more commonplace in academic literature from the 1990s on (Lepore, 2014). The increased attention that innovation research has drawn is due to the industries' demand. It has been widely recognized as a new "dimension" or "wave" sweeping through society, economy, and rivaling the magnitude of the Industrial Revolution, as well as an important mechanism for boosting economic growth. What perhaps best captures the essence of innovation as a multi-dimensional concept is the multitude of definitions that have been attached to it, either contemplating a specific aspect of it or simultaneously contemplating several of them. After conducting a thorough review of innovation literature published in the last few decades, Crossan and Apaydin (2010) synthesize the various definitions by defining innovation as both a process and an outcome. Thus, innovation is not interchangeable with technological advancement, as the latter is only affected by one of the several dimensions of innovation, namely technical/technological innovation. Nevertheless, other dimensions exercise considerable influence on innovation as well, such as leadership, managerial practice, administrative processes, and external factors. All these dimensions are grouped under a shared system in organizational settings in which the interconnectivity generates firm innovativeness. Hereinafter, the multi-faceted construct of organizational innovation is conceived.

1.1 The Perspective of Organizational Innovation

In a broader sense, organizational innovation refers to anything created or generated, within or adopted by an organization that is specifically new to that organization (Daft, 1978; Damanpour & Evan, 1984; Lam, 2004). Due to flexibility and lack of an exact and unique technical operational definition of "organizational innovation", its existing bulk of literature is highly diverse and does not invigorate a sound theoretical framework. Hence organizational innovation has been subject to various interpretations depending on the plethora of studies dedicated to its scientific kindred. Generally speaking, three different streams of the literature on organizational innovation have been identified by Lam (2004), each with its separate focus and questions addressed. First, organizational design theories concentrate on the link between organizational structure and its capacity to generate and/or enhance innovativeness (Albers Mohrman & Lawler III, 2014; Devereaux Jennings & Zandbergen, 1995; Lemus-Aguilar & Hidalgo, 2016; Longoni, Golini, & Cagliano, 2014; Mintzberg, 1979). Generally, this stream of research has been engulfed by the literature on technological innovation, aimed at explaining how structural features of innovative organizations affect their general product and process innovativeness. Second, theories of organizational cognition/learning mostly evolve around processes of knowledge acquirement and retention, and how such processes affect organizational innovativeness (Argyris & Schön, 1978; Lam, 2004; Nonaka, 1994; Nonaka & Takeuchi, 1995). Through these lenses, researchers ought to understand how organizations build capacities to exploit knowledge to induce innovation. Third, theoretical approaches concerning adaption and change are innately related to the previous stream, as they also are concerned with organizational processes that facilitate or inhibit organizational knowledge creation and retention, albeit from a different angle. They are mostly concerned with the capability of an organization to overcome hindrances and inertia when faced with environmental and/or technological shifts. Thus, this third perspective focuses on an organization's response to its external variables and their effects on it.

However, other distinctions within the field of organizational innovation can be identified. As Damanpour (1991) stated, organizational innovation has been characterized by studies in processes of innovation diffusion and adoption, as well as innovation generation (referred to as "innovating") and innovativeness, with the latter being a broader concept for a firm's innovation absorption capacity, notwithstanding its source. Thus, it is recognizable that an organization can either create, adopt or adapt innovation without having a particular influence on innovation generation and the mechanisms related to it. Nevertheless, despite the crude differences between conceptualizations of organizational innovation, real-life processes of firm innovativeness creation, adaption/adoption and retention are rudimentary, with a subtle degree of overlap between them. In a pioneering study, Damanpour (1991), building from earlier research on organizational innovation and recognizing the multitude of individual, organizational, and environmental influences on organizational innovation, recognized that the magnitude of studies of organizational variables' influence on organizational innovation is far greater compared to the other two. He identified 13 structural variables (such as specialization, functional differentiation) that exercised influence on organizational innovation and allocated them to four "moderating categories", namely type of organization, type of innovation, scope of innovation, and stage of adoption. The findings pinpointed that generally determinants of organizational innovation are relatively stable across different studies and that correction for sampling error is able to accommodate for the variance observed among studies. Furthermore, findings suggest that determinants of innovation were not significantly differentiated by any of the three types of innovation whereas moderator-determinant differences turned to be more relevant.

What this means is that a determinant can be crucial for moderating innovation in an organization based on contextual characteristics. For instance, determinants such as specialization and functional differentiation could be more relevant during the "stage of adoption" and when configured based on the "scope of innovation", compared to when accounting for differences in "types of organization" and "types of innovation". Hereupon, a Contingency Theory of Organizational Innovation took hold (Donaldson, 2001). In short, the Contingency Theory of Innovation states that innovation occurs in both organic and mechanistic organizational structures and that situational variables have the potential to significantly alter the organization's innovativeness capacity, in spite of an organization's level of innovativeness. According to Donaldson (1996, 2001), the Contingency Theory majorly contributes to the wealth of theories on organizational structure. It is based on the assumption that "*the most effective organizational structural design is where the structure fits contingencies*" (Donaldson,

2001). As organizational structure has the potential to affect innovation, the Contingency Theory of Organizational Structure became one of Innovation (Patwardhan, Ford, & Clarke, 2018).

However, moving away from the contingency model of explaining organizational innovation to a model that exercises greater focus on managerial role and non-technological aspects of innovation (Damanpour, Sanchez-Henriquez, & Chiu, 2018), further research on organizational innovation has examined to provide information related to the dual influence of internal, external knowledge and information sources on managerial innovations. Thus, the authors present managerial innovations as an essential force for attaining organizational effectiveness, but it is one that has been not properly assessed by academia. They state that academic research has mostly analyzed antecedents and consequences of both product and process innovation, especially in manufacturing firms, and that it has been heavily reliant upon easily accessible tools and measures such as patents, number of new products, number of employees and proportion of scientific and technician employees to that number, R&D expenditure, etc. (Armbruster et al., 2008; Damanpour & Aravind, 2011; Damanpour et al., 2018; Miles; 2005). Such an extensive focus on technological innovation has drained innovation research from non-technological processes and tools which in turn rendered research on strategic and managerial innovation, two primordial components of organizational innovation, scarce (Černe, Kaše, & Škerlavaj, 2016; Crossan & Apaydin, 2010; Damanpour et al., 2018; Keupp, Palmié, & Gassmann, 2012). Nevertheless, academic findings are promising and both internal and external mechanisms, such as knowledge sources and information channels, through which managerial and strategic innovation affect organizational innovation, are receiving more scrutiny from researchers due to their potential to propagate organizational innovation (Damanpour et al., 2018).

1.2 BID and Organizational Innovation

BID, in essence, is innovative thinking (Mitchell, 1999, 2001). As innovative structures have the capacity to enhance both service delivery and managerial practice, BIDs have incorporated some of these characteristics within their organizational framework. According to Mitchell (2001), an academic extensively involved with studies of BID-related innovation, BID represents a major innovation in the Public Administration sphere. First introduced in the 1980s in large

North American urban areas and later expanded worldwide, the establishment of BIDs represented a major shift in public policymaking and became a successful tool for instigating entrepreneurial innovation and management practices (which themselves are part of entrepreneurial innovation) in the public domain.

With its various administrative forms that it takes, which will be discussed later on in this monograph, BID constitutes a tool of empowerment (Briffault, 1999; Stahl, 2013) for various stakeholders including local government authorities, local SMEs, and other businesses, such as property and estate owners, tourism operators, and several other important beneficiaries. As all of these stakeholders come under a shared organizational structure, BID manifests a form of public-private partnership (Briffault, 1999; Grossman, 2008; Mitchell, 1999, 2001), which entails a common administration and asset ownership framework. In doing so, it introduces entrepreneurial principles to local government bureaucracy and offers businesses and local residents an opportunity for shared decision-making and day-to-day administration of the designed area. Structurally, as described by Mitchell (1999, 2001), BID represents a geographically defined majority of property owners and businesses that agree to impose a fee on all properties and businesses in their shared area to fund additional services, such as rehabilitation, cleaning, security, marketing, tourism development, and a host of other services. Local authorities intervene by establishing this district and then transferring funds to the BID organization, or an agreed representative. However, Stahl (2013) cites instances where BID has posed a threat of being exploited as a tool of majoritarian exploitation and imposition. Nevertheless, a further discussion of what BIDs are, what advantages and disadvantages they attain, will be explored further in the article.

According to Houston, Jr. (1997), BIDs enhance administrative innovation – a component of organizational innovation – in a way that combines entrepreneurial spirit, vision, and self-interest, with public finance and urban politics. By doing so, an innovative public-private hybrid organization umbrella forms in urban settings, blending managerial expertise with business-driven awareness and initiative. This is essentially the innovative component of organizational configuration that BID brings to public management and community leaders. It reinforces their roles as decision-makers and enables the establishment of various partnerships with the private sector that benefit both SMEs and residents. Hence, as Mitchell (2001) stated, innovation is quintessential to BID because of the way it is designed, providing an answer to many ills faced by modern urban areas, such as poor urban planning, hygiene standards, public transportation inefficiencies, mediocre marketing, and lack of adequate strategy for downtown SMEs. Similar to entrepreneurial initiatives, BIDs funnel managerial energy into the solution of problems, specifically public problems. In the following chapters, a more detailed description of the BID business model and commonly implemented organizational structures will follow.

2 A Literature Review on the Business Improvement District

2.1 The Concept of BID

Business Improvement District is an evolving and multidimensional concept. BIDs are found in districts where property or business owners voluntarily impose a tax on themselves to fund various projects in the area (Davies, 1997). In other words, the term BID describes a particular area where special funding mechanisms are used to provide additional services in order to improve the residential or business environment (Morçöl & Zimmermann, 2006). Taxes are usually collected by local government, and local government officials are always represented on the association besides area residents.

The associations take the form of non-profit corporations, created by local government (Unger, 2016), aiming to make public area improvements and provide special services as well (Davies, 1997). BIDs are in general initiated and governed by property owners and authorized by governments, whereas the term BID is used for both the selected area that receives special services and distinct investments and the association which governs this area (Morçöl, Zimmermann, Meek, & Hoyt, 2008). They deliver a highly adaptable small-scale management of urban spaces on the basis of the interests of property owners and businesses and to some degree substitute former public tasks.

BIDs stem from environmental policies that advocate for public-private partnerships (PPPs) in urban development (Unger, 2016). Hoyt and Gopal-Agge (2007) define BIDs as "privately directed and publicly sanctioned organizations that supplement public services within geographically defined boundaries by generating multiyear revenue through a compulsory assessment on local property owners and/or businesses". Therefore, the term BID is used to refer to both the geographical area and to the organizations that manage them. Morçöl and Zimmermann (2006) describe BIDs as publicly regulated but privately managed organizations that provide supplementary service to improve public area spaces. In many cases, BIDs are temporally limited and have to undergo a renewal process after a predetermined period of time. While there is a longer history of business and property owner associations in many countries, BIDs differ from the majority of the city management models (Michel & Stein, 2015). Once they are established, they are compulsory for all property owners or businesses in the given area and time. It is argued that this approach helps minimizing the problem of freeloaders known to voluntary associations, where those who do not participate in the funding process benefit nonetheless (McCann & Ward, 2010; Michel & Stein, 2015).

Through the establishment of BIDs, the private sector in essence provides public goods in the city center, such as road maintenance and security are provided through a supplemental tax paid by a business in the BID which they impose on, administer, and spend themselves (Tallon, 2013). In other words, the private sectors assume some of the functions formerly provided by the state with the aim to boost the local economy of the BID area.

Additionally, there are other terms besides "business improvement district", which refer to the same, or similar characteristics as BID does. Ward (2006) identifies "special improvement districts (SIDs)", "public improvement districts (PIDs)", "neighborhood improvement districts (NIDs)", "municipal improvement districts (MIDs)", and "business improvement districts (BIDs)" in the United States alone. The author identifies also "business improvement areas (BIAs)" in Canada, "downtown improvement districts (DIDs)" in Japan, "main street associations (MSAs)" in New Zealand, and "city improvement districts (CIDs)" in South Africa. In this list, we can only add "tourism improvement districts (TIDs)" recently introduced in Albania and which will be discussed in the following sections.

According to Mitchell (2008), BIDs are an innovation aimed at improving city's environmental conditions by providing small services which altogether improve the area while they share seven common attributes:

1   recognized by law,
2   created according to a process,
3   formed as an organization,
4   financed by a special assessment,
5   governed by a board,
6   managed by one person, and
7   reviewed periodically.

What is clearly evident is the aim of private companies at ensuring profitability in real estate and commercial activity in the city. Thus, property owners jointly act to create an attractive district and manage to keep it attractive. Whilst creating an attractive district, they manage to increase their profitability without depending (to a certain extent) on public services. Sager (2011) explains that these "business-friendly" *zones* are a set of developed controls separating land users in order to prevent negative external effects associated with the proximity of incompatible activities, achieving several urban planning goals, such as protection of natural and social environments, control urban expansion, and historical preservation. BIDs are a kind of "business-friendly" zones in an approach of controlling the emulated conditions within a business environment, or in other words, private management of public spaces (Sager, 2011).

In urban economics, zones are created to reduce the exposure of firms or households from cities' negative externalities including noise, glare, dust, odor, vibration, and smoke (O'Sullivan, 2012). The reasoning is that negative externalities cause inefficiencies for firms, thus reducing their profits. In the context of city businesses, noise, glare, dust, odor, vibration and smoke congestion, and parking conflicts are all negative externalities that can directly influence their activities. Therefore, the solution is to create a zone that eliminates these problems by creating a closed environment.

The creation of BIDs, in regard to negative externalities, generates a cost-benefit analysis. As BIDs are formed and maintained by an association of organizations, this imposes a cost on every firm that operates within the area. The benefits that the firm attains begin from the reduced exposure of negative externalities and end with the added services from collected taxes. For these to happen, a number of businesses in a BID need to be considerable, so from the economies of scale the cost of service per firm is at the lowest, and the profit from the service and the reduced externalities is at the highest. On the other hand, the size of the zone cannot exceed a certain benchmark, as most externalities rather than diminishing, increase, posing additional costs to firms (O'Sullivan, 2012).

From the perspective of municipalities, another motivation for zoning is to ensure that firms generate a fiscal surplus (Calabrese, Epple, & Romano, 2007; Fischel, 2004). BIDs are usually voluntary organizations created by businesses, but sometimes they are incentivized by local governments in the process of urban planning and land control. For ensuring that businesses create a fiscal surplus, local governments incentivize the creation of BIDs, as most of the services in the area are financed by the fund of the additional assessment and few are financed by local taxes.

Through limiting the environment, unlike a country or a city economic development and strategic planning of a large geographical area, BIDs focus their managerial expertise and allocate their resources only on this environment. By doing so, they become an alternative to traditional municipal planning. Mitchell (2001) lists some of the main characteristics regarding BIDs:

- BIDs are usually established through a petition process by a number of businesses in a specific block where the initiative may come from real estate developers, property owners, businesses, local government, or other associations;
- BIDs receive most of their funding from an added assessment on the businesses and property owners located in the geographical area, but they can receive additional funds in the form of development grants, donations, and subsidies from the local government and/or the state budget;
- BIDs can implement services through non-profit organizations, public-private (in form of nonprofit) partnerships and government agencies;
- BIDs create their development strategies and focus on what will be the most effective for the business district. The strategies establish a direction for the activities and services, while the governing board manages the district and maintains accountability. There is actually a limited role the local government can play in the operation and the management of a BID, expect to monitor financials and collect assessments while allowing the board to have autonomy of decision and flexibility.

In the institutional approach, Unger (2016) recognizes three main public responsibilities: (i) the primary function to carry out the public attribute to tax and to spend; (ii) provision of a wide range of supplemental services, and (iii) they seek to implement in their district the broad perception of improving the general environment. Each BID is governed by a designated commercial area (DMA), (BID is actually the informal term used for the organization), which is governed by an elected board.

BIDs are assigned by the local government to manage a district or a geographic area, yet that management is governed by BID's private board (Unger, 2016). The board of directors exercises a series of functions in a BID (Cook, 2009): they are responsible for designing, developing, and authorizing new projects while out-sourcing the implementation for servicing, budget supervision, project management, and BID promotion to a partner. This clearly shows the public and private partnership character of a BID, but also highlights the private bias of it. A BID has its own budget and in control of its allocation. Thus, for a given period of time, the board decides to prioritize the budget in a number of services or otherwise in the entirety of projects in the area. The taxation mechanism is in fact a combination of private and public power, as the taxes are collected by local government and then fully redistributed to the BID. In this case, the power of the local government is reduced to the channeling of taxes from the business to the BID, which again shows the limited public role BIDs have.

Lloyd, McCarthy, McGreal, and Berry (2003) have described the process through which a BID is established. It starts with a piece of legislation passed by government authorities that authorizes the establishment of a BID, usually preceded by a petition process or another form of local initiative whereby various stakeholders such as businesses, estate owners, local governments, tourism associations, or any other interested developer lead to the legislative initiative for establishing the BID. As soon as this first process is accomplished, the second process – which requires voting on the proposed BID design – takes place. The required majority may vary depending on the type of proposal from 51 to 70%. Third, the agreed-upon assessment is collected on property owners and businesses, which is then used to implement services by means of non-profit organization, government corporation, or a public-private partnership. Finally, the board is accountable for BID activities, and also the local government supervises the role of BID.

Morçöl and Wolf (2010) explain four different conceptualizations of BIDs in the literature. Most commonly, BIDs have public-private partnership character, where the private association cooperates in the network mode with the governance at the local level. BIDs can be tools for government policies, or instruments of implementing wider policy goals, whether promoting welfare or provision of local goods and products. Beside policy tools, BIDs can take the form of a quasi-governmental entity of not having a hierarchical relationship with the government and not having the government as a source of funding but providing a variation from the policy tools incentivized by the government.

Furthermore, BIDs can act as "private governments" or as actors of urban governance networks. As Morçöl and Wolf (2010) suggest, there is a wide range of BIDs, which can in fact have distinguishing differences from one another. Briffault (1999) claims that BIDs are a mark of public and private combination with local government characteristics: small-sized, more opportunities for associates to voice their views, control their contributions, participate in public life, and have complete information about the processes.

These kinds of working partnerships create substantial public benefits, such as improved services, cost saving for the local governments, and risk management with the private sector, whilst promoting efficiencies in public service delivery (Hastings, 1996). In the context of a partnership, Peel, Lloyd, and Lord (2009) identify five imperatives that can strengthen the collaboration: (i) establishing a shared vision; (ii) efficiently using the available resources; (iii) jointly addressing difficulties in policy or service environments; (iv) strengthening their position in a policy or service area; and (v) resolving conflict. These conditions do not necessarily constitute a blueprint of successful partnerships of BIDs, but they rather express important notions upon the formation of a BID.

2.2 History and Perspectives

The first BID was created in Toronto, Canada, in 1970, as local retailers of a small shopping area realized that voluntary contributions were not going to be enough for them to deliver their annual improvement strategies (Ward, 2007). Thus, the decision was taken with the inclusion of local officials to establish a self-imposed tax. With the power to tax members, the BID model of Toronto represents a persistent, competitive, and flexible strategy to confront local dilemmas through the provision of additional public services (Hoyt, 2008).

Despite these Canadian origins, it is the US model of city and town center management that expanded the notion as a policy option for urban management, or as Ward (2006) claims, it finally caught the attention of the world and especially Europe and UK policymakers. Unlike Canada, there was no state encouragement to create Business Improvement Districts, while the legal system meant that every time a place wanted to establish a Business Improvement District it had to get state legislative approval (Ward, 2007). As a result, only about one-third of the USA's Business Improvement Districts were established before 1990. According to several estimates (Morçöl et al., 2008), as of the late 1990s, there were 800 to 1,200 BIDs in Canada and the United States. In 2007, there were estimated to be over 750 BIDs in the United States, over 400 in Canada, over 350 in Europe, and over 60 in the United Kingdom. BIDs are growing in South Africa (50), Japan (290),

Australia (200), and New Zealand (180) as well as in France, Belgium, and Germany (Grossman, 2010).

BIDs were introduced in the UK in 2004 by the "New Labor" government (Tallon, 2013). The first BID introduced in the UK was Kingston First. It was elected in 2004 and opened in 2005 in the center of Kingston upon Thames, an outer borough of London and three years later the first BIDs in Scotland were voted in (Ward & Cook, 2014). By the end of 2012, there were 145 BIDs in operation in the UK, with 126 in England, 17 in Scotland, and only two in Wales (Ward & Cook, 2014). The city with the largest concentration of BIDs in the UK is London with recently more than 50 BIDs (*The Evolution of London's Business Improvement Districts*, 2016).

Briffault (1999) explains that the public choice arguments regarding the efficient delivery of public services by a private organization and that the public sector was unnecessary in a large number of service delivery led policymakers in the United States and other countries to launch large-scale privatization policies in the 1980s. BIDs were among the respondents to economic conditions and public policy changes in the following decades as the economic direction of the 1980s was focused on privatization policies and abandonment of urban areas (Davies, 1997; Morçöl et al., 2008).

Thus, BIDs emerged as a response to the limiting public policies and services in urban areas, as businesses perceived that more services were necessary to improve their environment and their profitability. As Briffault (1999) describes it, in a time where neither the government nor the voters wanted new taxes, BIDs were created to impose additional taxes, with the businesses subject to taxation taking the policymaking role in establishing the BIDs. From the European perspective at first glance, BIDs seem to be just another aspect of the privatized American City that is frequently constructed as the antipode to the idea (or ideology) of the "European City", that is, a historical and dense city of civic emancipation and public space (Michel & Stein, 2015).

On the other hand, Peyroux, Pütz, and Glasze (2012) argue that BIDs include elements of the entrepreneurial urban politics, as the establishment of a new configuration of partnership that increases the role of the private actors, the role of the local and sub-municipal scale, and different dimensions of privatization. BIDs are a specific form of public-private partnership and of "networked local governance" in which the boundaries between the public and the private spheres become fluid. The strengthening of private actors goes along with an increased importance of the local political scale linked to the devolution and downscaling of central government functions. Thus, in a way, they deliver public services privately, within their environment.

Furthermore, BIDs were created partly because of the differences in terms of the level of services between cities and suburbs in the United States as users expressed a preference for cleaner, safer environments of suburban malls (Lloyd et al., 2003). What followed was that cities began to take action to develop their services and environmental quality to match suburb's standards. It was not only US cities that had these issues, as the population was leaving cities for the suburbs and stores had to either be reallocated in shopping malls or go out of business, and as it was the rich population which moved from the cities, the purchasing power of cities declined (Ward, 2007).

Besides, there existed a wider problem of under-investment in regeneration of urban area, or increased investments from the local government, which completed the spiral of decline together with the lack of quality services (Judd, 2003; Lloyd et al., 2003). The capital investments in tourism and entertainment facilities, as far as the city budgets could afford, did not solve all the problems. They were not sufficient to attract tourists or suburbanites to downtowns because most of them were not esthetically attractive and most of them were not even safe (Judd, 2003).

In urban economics, firms cluster to exploit agglomeration economies including localization economies at the industry level and urbanization economies at the city level or as O'Sullivan (2012) suggests, firms may cluster:

- to share a supplier of an intermediate input subject to economies of scale;
- to share a labor pool if the variation in product demand is greater at the firm level than at the industry level;
- to provide better skill matches, leading to higher productivity;
- because people and firms are attracted to cities as they facilitate knowledge spillovers, learning, and social opportunities.

Thus, businesses within a BID can exploit these advantages even if the BID is composed only of shopping malls. Sharing an intermediate input supplier would be enough to stimulate the grouping of the firms. As the urban developments of the 80s might be the reason for initial clustering and the creation of BIDs, the agglomeration economies are the reason for the further development and enlargement of BIDs, as it took different forms and incorporated diverse businesses within.

As it spread across countries, local governments realized that this provided means of funding services and improvement in public areas without raising general taxes, or as Briffault (1999) suggested, it tackled two problems simultaneously: they provided means of solving the free-rider problem that plagues the efforts of chambers of commerce and merchants associations to raise funds to pay for services for their areas, while directing the spending on the programs and projects they want which would be controlled by their representatives. Mitchell (2008) supports these two arguments as too, while also adding three more: (i) the association could cooperate with quasi-government entities, development agencies, and other authorities to deliver joint effort in improving the district; (ii) the association had, besides financial, legal ability to deliver services without deepening on the financial or political stability of the governments; and (iii) the association has responsibility for the development of the district.

BIDs are now a contemporary development in urban delivery tools by combining the framework of state-market relations to provide collective outcomes in public settings. Peel et al. (2009) argue that these developments are a major relief to local (and central) governments which avoid, to a certain extent, urban planning and the cost accompanied with it. In order for these partnerships to be effective, there needs to be a good definition of private property rights, public property rights, and the clear distinction between private and public property. This involves defining the legal and contractual relations between the BID, as an entity, and the local government by defining the full extent of the administrative processes and also the economic relations in providing services and securing the perceived public interest.

The clear definition of the relationship between the government and the private sector, or between public and private property, is essential to separate the interests of the BID. Such interests are the local interest or the public interest. Needham and Louw (2006) regard the rules that regulate these partnerships around the legal rights, and economic resources are clearly identified in the government policy framework as important. The pooled private resources of members to address the unique needs of commercial subsections are regarded as potentially efficient distributive tools, thus empowering the private sector and limiting the public sector (Gross, 2013).

In the context of BIDs, the current balance between the managerial and democratic or participatory roles of local governments could be outlined as emphasizing citizens' choice between different service providers in a market-based approach but under some public control

(Pierre, 1998). Thus, the issue is no longer about who is in charge of the public services, but whether the services offered match the quality demanded by the customers, and in a broader sense, the citizens. When this is the case, BIDs as a mixed delivery approach, represent a middle stand that can address the needs of the citizens for more efficient services and avoid all or nothing contracting based on public choice (Warner & Hefetz, 2007).

The increasing acceptance, in both planning and politics, of BIDs as an instrument of city center development goes hand in hand with a particular perception and social construction of problems as well as with specific ways of defining the purpose of urban policy and designing solutions to resolve these problems (Mitchell, 2001). This has far-reaching consequences for the design and use of urban spaces, as well as for the ways in which public services are understood and delivered by public actors themselves. This holds as the reallocation of decision-making powers in neighborhood development and the processes of privatization encourage the commodification of spaces within city centers and suburban centers (Peyroux et al., 2012).

Grossman (2010) describes BIDs as a form of "sub governmental" institutions, referring to public institutions governing a particular area established to address specific needs of the community that cannot be addressed adequately by internal government programs. The author explains that sub governments are limited on their purposes and are specially authorized to permit government often to proceed into previously non-governmental areas of society that require collective action. This can consequently imply that sub governments can engage private sector interests and act as a mechanism to coordinate those interests with a public purpose.

The sub governmental view of BIDs may be correct to a certain extent, but there are certain issues regarding accountability that conflict this view. Unger (2016) identifies that the problem with the concept of the local government being in most cases the advocate for establishment of BIDs, and at the same time also the institution which is supposed to monitor them, can certainly be conflictual. Judd (2003) suggests that BIDs are mechanism in order to bypass normal democratic processes to achieve economic development in urban areas, as they make choices and implement commercial revitalization policies relatively distant from the traditional public policy. As the author explains these institutions were not bound by the rules that discouraged public initiatives by general-purpose governments; they could protect their information and books from public scrutiny, but at the same time, since they pursued public objectives, they could act just like governments and generate revenue, receive funds from other governments, and borrow money and sell tax-free bonds.

Furthermore, there is reason to state that there is a broader political rationale motivating governments to turn to the private sector to manage public works. Adams (2007) claims that placing responsibility outside of elected government helps to isolate public works from political challenges that may come from taxpayers and citizens, particularly if the projects have high costs and serve only to a small segment of the population. In a democratic system, elected representatives are accountable to the public for their decisions and activities. The issue of accountability underlies the notion of one person, one vote; however, constitutional issue apart, the question of accountability here is essentially a matter of the cities government willingness to engage in a system for regularly monitoring BIDs (Briffault, 1999). Not only are the decisions made by independent businesses beyond direct influence by the voting public, but they are also often made behind closed doors.

Local governments are supposed to oversee BID operations. By definition, the state-enabling laws usually require BID boards to submit annual reports to their local governments, and local governments are supposed to approve their annual budgets. Morçöl and Wolf (2010) claim that even though some local governments do use their oversight authorities seriously, in most other cases, annual BID reports and sunset provisions are mere formalities that local governments ignore.

Even though the importance of private contributions is the key ingredient in completing public projects, it comes with the long-term price of explicit private control through a public authority (Landow & Ebdon, 2012). BIDs possess power ranging from the authority to operate a community court to the acquisition of state-federal funds (Mitchell, 2001). Considering this, BIDs are criticized for being autonomous legal entities that are not accountable for the district's residents, the jurisdiction in which they operate, or the BID's business or property owner constituents (Briffault, 1999). The possession of (private) control implies that BID activities are likely to impact a certain group of interest, which makes BIDs accountable to three major stakeholders (Hochleutner, 2003):

1 the local property or business owners subject to BID assessments (Owners);
2 residents of the BID (BID Residents); and
3 residents of the municipality (City Residents).

Although there are arguments that BIDs are accountable as long as certain measures, such as annual reports, external audits, and authorization requirements are delivered (Morçöl & Wolf, 2010), to compile a public account of their activities, they need to prove their worth to participating property owners and the general public, BIDs need to implement and monitor performance indicators like customer surveys, crime rates, occupancy rates, retail sales, number of jobs created, and pedestrian counts (Hoyt & Gopal-Agge, 2007).

Moreover, to the extent that BIDs exercise governmental power, their small size limits the number of the BID's constituents and makes it easier for those constituents to monitor BID activities, measure BID performance, and respond when BID officials act improperly (Hochleutner, 2003). Regarding performance, Mitchell (2008) suggests that by working collaboratively with the local governments and the business associations and because there are many external factors that affect the economy in an urban area, it is difficult to measure the impact of BIDs in the area.

2.3   Role and Significance

The most important role BIDs have is the improvement of their environment through supplemental local service delivery, capital improvements, promotion, and marketing. Mitchell (2001) on the study of BID operations delivers a list of the services in which managers of BIDs are involved mostly, captured by a nationwide survey of managers in the US. The service managers were mostly involved in consumer marketing, producing festivals and events, coordinating sales promotion, or producing maps and newsletters. Additionally, they were involved in parking and transportation services. Service managers were also involved in capital improvements. Fourth, they were involved in public advocacy, or in promoting policies to the community, lobbying government on behalf of business interest and other. Furthermore, the list continues as follows: public space regulation; providing security; economic development or offering incentives (such as tax abatements or loans) to new and expanding businesses, and lastly, social services in the form of aiding the homeless, providing job training, and supplying youth services. Another interesting conclusion of the author is that city size explains differences in service delivery patterns of BIDs. BIDs from largest cities were more likely to be involved in the entire range of services or the range of consumer marketing and maintenance.

Following Mitchell (2008) and Morçöl et al. (2008) we can summarize BIDs service delivery as follows:

1 Consumer marketing (festivals, events, self-promotion, maps, newsletters)
2 Economic development (tax abatements and loans to new businesses)
3 Policy advocacy (promoting public policies, lobbying)
4 Maintenance (trash collection, litter removal, washing sidewalks, etc.)
5 Parking and transportation (public parking systems, maintaining transit shelters)
6 Security (security guards, electronic security systems, cooperating with police)
7 Social services (aiding homeless, providing job training, youth services)
8 Capital improvements (street lighting, street furniture, trees, shrubbery)
9 Strategic planning (the design of public spaces)
10 Public space regulation (managing vendors, panhandlers, and vehicle loading)
11 Establishing and operating community courts

Most of the services are basically public services often offered by most of the local governments, but some of the services make the BIDs important for the development of the area. There are a lot of services that have a bigger impact on the improvement of the SMEs within the district, which can be difficult to receive when they are not part of a district, such as parking and transportation, security, maintenance, and of course capital improvements.

There are further services that characterize BIDs. Business loans are more accessible when the business is part of the association, which in turn makes it easier for the small and medium businesses to increase their potential. There is strategic planning which specifically designs the role and vision for every business within the district, as well as their long-term strategy of development. Policy advocacy is another service that is quite impossible to be reached by SMEs without this integration. In this way, SMEs can access funds from governments and other development entities, mostly for the improvement of their environment, a case that will be further investigated in the next section.

According to Mitchell (2008) BID can improve the prospect of cities in four diverse approaches:

1   BIDs proceed from the assumption that small-scale planning is more sensitive to community needs than city broad-based land clearance and large-scale redevelopment projects.
2   BIDs contradict suburban development and draw substance from the critique of suburban life and the popularity of growth management policies.
3   BIDs are part of a philosophy that administrative fragmentation helps rather than hinders the modern city.
4   BIDs are linked to the economic development policy mania (at least according to the author in American cities) and to the conviction that the public interest is best advanced through the entrepreneurial activities of public-private partnership.

In the context of the institutional economics, there have been several developments that constitute the efficiency and effectiveness of public and private institutions. In the previous section, we discussed the importance of the definition of the private and public property as important in maintaining a clear separation between public and private interests. There is a more profound aspect when it comes to the clear definition of property rights, and in this case, service delivery as well.

Needham and Louw (2006) recognizes the importance of these institutional forms in the reduction of transaction costs. In this view, there is a clear efficiency in collecting taxes as the BIDs are easier to control by their board. Entry and exit policies are clear to all members, in which case not providing the assessments is clearly an exit benchmark. Even though the assessment is collected by the local authorities, the BIDs have clear access to the process of collection which prevents possible flows in the process. The last step to the transfer of the assessments in the complete control of the BIDs is the final transaction between the BID and the local government. As it goes to the BIDs, these funds are expected to be efficiently allocated, as the BID is in this instance a clearly private and profit-maximizing institution.

Transaction costs are relatively low due to the service management of the BIDs. As they demand efficiency and are able to control the process of service delivery, there are no bureaucratic and corruptive issues to cause inefficiencies. Geuting (2007) argues that there is in fact a correlation between the transfer of partnerships rights and the speed of development as well as to the improvement quality in the medium and long run.

He also explains the convenience of these partnerships. Besides facilitating a positive business environment these partnerships also encourage private-sector investments and development. This is certainly deductive as a more efficient environment would produce more profitable businesses, which consequently will increase their investments and improve their services.

On the other hand, Warner and Hefetz (2007) suggest that while contracting other organizations to provide public services it poses an additional transaction costs due to the principal dilemma in whether it is more efficient to deliver the services internally or to outsource them to the market. There are possible costs of information asymmetries that add to the transaction costs (Warner & Hefetz, 2007), which result from the contractual framework and the legal boundaries in which BIDs are allowed to operate.

The problem is not the profitability of the businesses within the BIDs. They are interested in delivering good service to increase their profits, but there are public services that can limit the concept of public space. Most BIDs operate in public spaces, thus the services they provide must not violate basic public space rights for the citizens. It is hard to control them if the services delivered to the businesses limit the concept of the public space if the contractual design does allow leaks (Hefetz & Warner, 2004). However, a good contractual framework and clear definition of boundaries between the BIDs and the local government would eliminate this issue.

Furthermore, the assumption following the establishment of such institutions in partnership with the local government and the "fragmentation" of local governance is that this framework will create a more efficient, inclusive, and pluralist local governance by joining different economic actors to identify top priorities, needs, and work to provide them (Geddes, 2006). The institutional approach suggests that an efficient outcome in planning and management comes from a proper arrangement of responsibilities, incentives, and ownership, which involves cooperation by both private and public actors to secure effective and efficient allocation of resources (Peel et al., 2009). Into the context of BIDs, efficiency in delivering services is a clear advantage.

Privatization theory normally assumes a dualist perspective. It argues that private providers deliver public services more efficiently because they operate in more competitive markets and respond to these forces better. This results in private organizations behaving less formally and less bureaucratically than government agencies (Unger, 2016). For example, the private sector is more autonomous in decision making, whereas government bureaucrats are supposed to act within a procedural framework, limiting flexibility and speed of decision. This supports the claim that private organizations have more potential in responding more quickly and effectively to any issue that arises, whether operational or administrative (Warner & Hefetz, 2007).

In addition, efficiency improvements are also partly from the prevention of the "free-riders" problem. This problem consists of a market failure that occurs where businesses take advantage of being able to use a common service or public good, without paying for it (Briffault, 1999). The mechanism used to prevent this problem is the creation and the maintenance of a dedicated and secure source of funding (Mitchell, 1999), or at the very least, the services being provided within an exclusive area.

While it may be clear that private delivery of public services may be more efficient, the cases of BIDs are special. For most of their services, they do not take part in a competitive environment besides the constant competitiveness for grants from governmental funds and other entities. They have a quasi-guaranteed revenue and a high degree of autonomy. In their continued existence it is not important to be efficient, which poses the question if BIDs can be seen as a private profit-maximizing organization or government-like organization, less competitive and more bureaucratic (Warner & Hefetz, 2007). Previously, Pierre (1998) argued that once private organization partners with the municipal government it no longer needs to respond only to market forces, which softens the notion of BIDs as private organizations.

The structure of BIDs is formed by businesses interested and involved in addressing problems and finding solutions, which, as previously discussed provides a wide range of advantages in terms of effectiveness of service delivery. Therefore, BIDs tend to stimulate a certain degree of entrepreneurship and innovation (MacDonald, 1996; Mitchell, 2001). The fact that businesses form a closed environment, the chance that creative and innovative ideas are spread from one business to another is high, and in most cases stimulates the general innovation within the BID. BIDs allow local businesses an independent power to act to introduce a range of local improvements, in terms of physical improvement and service improvement (Berry, Godfrey, McGreal, & Adair, 2010). Local businesses can introduce ideas and can propose solutions to the common problems as well as to their specific issues as they have their representatives on the board. This level of local democracy, together with a certain level of internal competition, can create an environment that stimulate innovation within the BIDs.

Lloyd et al. (2003) extend the importance of BIDs to the creation of social capital, compromising norms, and networks of trust and reciprocity, which can accelerate economic development and enhance competitiveness. Theories suggest that from investing in social capital, or social relations with expected returns, the benefits belong to the whole group that take part in these social relations (Lin, 2017). The institutional structure of BIDs is appropriate for accelerating social capital by means of networking, cooperation for common goals, and building trust through continuous relations (Lloyd et al., 2003). In addition to this, by investing in social capital the governance of BIDs becomes easier as the relationships within the members of the board, representatives from businesses, and business owners are strengthened leading the decision-making process to become more effective.

2.4 BIDs and Urban Regeneration

Urban regeneration is a widely experienced phenomenon as most towns and cities have been involved in regeneration schemes with the participation of many economic agents from local governments to development companies. Nevertheless, urban regeneration is little understood. Urban regeneration is the outcome of the interchange between processes that drive physical, social, environmental, and economic transition, and it is also a response to the opportunities and challenges which are presented by urban degeneration in a particular place and specific point in time (Roberts, 2008). Each urban area, town, or city faces challenges that are likely to require the construction and implementation of a specific response to achieve urban regeneration. Additionally, (Roberts, 2008) defines urban regeneration as a "comprehensive and integrated vision and action which leads to the resolution of urban problems and which seeks to bring about a lasting improvement in the economic, physical, social and environmental condition of an area that has been subject to change".

Towns and cities develop over time in a process of change, which is both inevitable and can be argued as beneficial (McCarthy, 2007). The pressure to change land uses can come about for a number of reasons, whether it be changes in the economy, environment, social need, or a combination of these, thus becoming inevitable. Besides, it is beneficial because forces of change create opportunities to adjust and improve the conditions of towns and cities. Regeneration in its most basic form can be understood as "action to address need", where need refers to the need to resolve problems as a result of market failure and subsequent job loss and disinvestment (Granger, 2010).

The process of urban regeneration is multidimensional. Economic regeneration is a vital part of the process of urban regeneration. It counters the economic decline experience of cities with the changes in the employment structure and increasing globalization (Noon, Smith-Canham, & Eagland, 2000). One of the most common examples is the rise of entrepreneurialism in the 1980s represented by the neoliberal philosophy involving deregulation, liberalization, and privatization. The social need was largely subordinated to the needs of businesses. During this period of urban regeneration policy, the emphasis was put on property-led initiatives and the creation of an entrepreneurial culture, while urban entrepreneurialism became the main form of governance of cities globally (Tallon, 2013).

BIDs were amongst the entrepreneurial forms of governance that evolved during the period when cities were focused on production readjustment of other economic structures. They embodied all the characteristics of urban regeneration at the time: displacement or transfer of power to non-elected agencies, deregulation of urban planning or property-led regeneration, the encouragement of partnership between public and private actors, and privatization (Tallon, 2013). In this context, BIDs emerge to further advance urban regeneration in the form of a new partnership between businesses, public sector, and not-for-profit agencies, by transforming the environment and reforming the urban governance in order to attract mobile capital and investments in the city (Jonas & McCarthy, 2010).

In the process of urban regeneration, the physical appearance and the environmental quality of cities and neighborhoods are highly regarded as symbols of the quality of life, progress, and prosperity (Jeffrey & Pounder, 2000). As the authors explain, physical renewal is usually a necessary if not sufficient condition for successful regeneration and in some circumstances it may be the main engine of regeneration, while in almost all cases it is an important visible sign of commitment to change and improvement.

In the framework of urban regeneration and the physical appearance and environmental quality of cities, BIDs are particularly capable of creating the necessary conditions for this to happen. From the BIDs services mentioned in the previous section, there are some, such as maintenance and capital improvements that are directly related to the physical regeneration of the area. They have increased their importance in cities as preferred destinations and in some cities, they have created the image of a landmark (Morçöl, Vasavada, & Kim, 2014). Urban regeneration in the context of physical appearance and environmental quality is also related to cities increasingly relying on city marketing to increase investments, tourism, and residency (Kavaratzis, 2004), which will be further discussed in the following section.

In the further process of urban regeneration, BIDs take a more important role. As in a broader sense they are business communities and influence the process of urban regeneration by creating job possibilities for the local community. Trebeck (2007) views the private sector as the main contributor in the regeneration, in the extent of financial, natural, social, physical, and human capital. In the extent of human capital, the author suggests that the private sector is the main source of job creation in a city.

While spreading the entrepreneurial culture and the innovative business ways led by the private market (Tallon, 2013), BIDs stimulate a labor demand for skilled and unskilled works as the range of businesses situated in these areas focuses on a variety of products. The more specialized the general focus of the BIDs, for example, technology-based businesses, the more they will attract highly skilled labor. The urban regeneration process requires that the labor market provides jobs for a wide range of skills, provides training and education (Johnston & Hart, 2000).

The other approach to regeneration is the cultural policy perspective or the idea that a city needs specific local assets such as cultural facilities, services, and locations, as well as a provision for high technology (Comunian, 2011). This encourages a creative and innovative class that interacts with the "cultural city" and highly skilled professionals to jointly enhance the entrepreneurial culture of the city (Comunian, 2011). As Miles and Paddison (2005) claim "Culture is a source of prosperity and cosmopolitanism in the process of international urban competitiveness through hosting international events and centers of excellence, inspiring creativity and innovation, driving high growth business sectors such as creative industries, commercial leisure and tourism, and increasing profile and name recognition". The emerging culture class is distinct from the service sector class because they are primarily paid to create rather than to execute orders and are typified by very high levels of education and human capital (Jones & Evans, 2008).

Renewal and regeneration programs have contributed to the entrepreneurial culture of the city, focused on the dynamic combination of cultural atmosphere, sense of enthusiasm, creativity and regenerated physical environment, cultural facilities, and materialized creativity, lead the regeneration of urban spaces and economies (Ponzini & Rossi, 2010). In this context, the approach of the urban policies toward BIDs has evolved from simple business and retail centers to entrepreneurial setting, full of creative and innovative businesses, which lead the entrepreneurial culture of the city (Ward, 2010).

BIDs have the potential to achieve a range of regeneration outcomes, but Lloyd et al. (2003) suggest a number of operational problems in the policy implementation of BIDs in the process of regeneration: first there is the issue of integration of BIDs with other mechanisms for service delivery as well as other policy mechanisms in relation to urban regeneration. In other words, will the businesses in the district be willing to accept an increased level of taxation for what they will perceive as potential benefits? Second, there is the issue of the expectations businesses have from the provision of core services by the government; third there is the problem of different taxation regimes.

Another important concept in the study of the role of a business district and the effect of its spillovers is the extent to which agglomeration economies occur. Such economies arise from the geographic proximity of similar, technologically advanced enterprises. The presence of business districts, as leaders in both technological and capital accumulation, will serve to further stimulate the possibility for agglomeration in such locations (Driffield, 2001). This will serve to increase the potential for technology transferal and therefore improvements in the technological capabilities of domestic businesses. The non-technological advantages, such as managerial abilities, the exploitation of scale economies, or superior coordination of resources, if adopted by the whole country industry may bring performance improvements as well (Driffield, 2001).

There are some drawbacks to urban regeneration and its entrepreneurialism legacy. Tallon (2013) carefully summarized the major criticisms of urban regeneration:

- The definition of the urban problem and the scale of the response: urban policies were focused on the symptoms of the problems (de-industrialization, unemployment, poverty, social exclusion, and growing inequalities) rather than the causes. The government responses to the problems faced by the cities were quite small in comparison to other governmental spending, allocating an abundance of issues in the hands of the local government.
- The fragmentation of policy and lack of co-ordination: too many government departments responsible for urban policy and it develops into bureaucracy and complexity with few resources to match the scale of the attendant problems.
- The lack of a long-term strategic approach: related to the lack of co-ordination and coherence of urban policy was the view that it

also lacked long-term strategic objectives; policies were seen as pragmatic and programmatic rather than demonstrating strategic thinking relating to changing cities and city-regions, short-term, relative to the longstanding nature and depth of the problems being addressed.

- The over-reliance on property-led regeneration: the mode of urban regeneration relied heavily on policy instruments that aimed to attract the private sector to invest in property in run-down urban areas on the assumption that this would result in local economic regeneration and that the benefits would trickle down to deprived communities; the approach overlooks human resource issues, such as education and training, the underlying competitiveness of production, and investment in essential infrastructure.

2.5 BIDs in the Framework of City Marketing and City Branding

The process of the regeneration of the physical appearance and environmental quality are key factors in constructing what Paddison (1993) defined as *city marketing*, the promotion of a city, or a district within the city, with the aim of altering the external perceptions of the city in order to encourage tourism or enable business relocation. Cities are increasingly relying on city marketing methods to compete for inward investments, tourism revenues, and residents, while the marketing target focuses on services rather than goods.

Entrepreneurialism captures the sense in which cities are being run in a more business-like manner, with local governments embracing business characteristics, such as risk taking, inventiveness, promotion, and profit motivation (Kavaratzis, 2004). This is only a natural consequence of such an entrepreneurial governance. In order to face competition, urban management must be applied in the entrepreneurial sense; it must be strategic, market-oriented, and able to respond to the trend for increasing competition and interdependence.

In order to face competition, urban management must be done with much more competitiveness and entrepreneurial sense. It must be strategic and market-oriented, able to respond to trends of increasing competition, and interdependence between cities that derive from the globalized economies with an implied increase in the scale of economic relationships between cities (Liouris & Deffner, 2005). Graham (2002) continues on the line of the entrepreneurial cities, by outlining two important notions, "external city" and "internal city". The "external city" is the superficial area which can be summarized by landmarks and signature buildings, whereas the "internal city" is the city of mind, or the inner-directed *mnemonic city*, one that is concerned with social inclusion and exclusion, lifestyle, diversity, and multiculturalism.

Both of the notions can be used as commodities to promote the city. The level of development of the "external" or "internal" city will also determine the nature of city promotion, as the "two cities" are not always coexisting simultaneously. They can collude or interact (Graham, 2002). The "external city", in the context of marketing, will be able to promote the city with the aim of improving tourism, and to a certain extent, investments, whilst the "internal city" image will be able to promote the business environment and entrepreneurial culture, attract investments, residents, and develop the city in the long term. Kavaratzis (2004) implies that the crucial point for the management and marketing of the city is the point of interaction as it is the point of the overall perception of the city formed by each individual with comes to encounter the city.

Another important concept evolved from city marketing, *city branding*. There were two important factors that caused the shift from city marketing to city branding (Kavaratzis, 2007): first it was the growing importance of the image in determining the people who use the city, whether investors, developers, visitors or residents; second the image of the city and the attempt to influence it could provide the necessary way to coordinate the marketing target activities to aim at. The importance of the image for the user of the place is the way they sense, understand, use, and connect with the place (Kavaratzis & Ashworth, 2005). Moreover, the authors identify that a place needs to be differentiated through unique brand, recognized as existing, perceived in the minds of place customers as possessing superior qualities to competitors and thereby offering a superior positioning.

In an increasingly growing and competitive global market, destinations create a unique identity to differentiate themselves from competitors. People have a desire to experience elements that they subjectively desire and focus on achieving hedonic experiences when they travel and therefore when searching for a destination to travel to, they search for locations that are positioned, in their mind, as unique and possess the greatest potential to meet their criteria for an enjoyable experience (Godfrey & Gretzel, 2016). Destinations are marketed in ways that promote a positive image in the minds of their audience.

Destination branding incorporates the traditional and non-traditional approaches of the marketing discipline with particular focus on branding strategies for promotion, development, and enhancement of salability of a particular place or region toward its prospective customers that include tourists, investors (including FDIs), students, and exports (Bose, Roy, & Tiwari, 2016). Even from a theoretical point of view, the main and broadly defined target groups in place marketing and place branding are (1) visitors; (2) residents and workers; and (3) business and industry (Zanker & Braun, 2010).

One of the most important outcomes of city marketing and city branding is the attraction of investments in the city, which can take the form of native direct investments or foreign direct investments. This can become of imperative importance in the economic development of the city if they are in the creative and innovative industries (Jacobsen, 2009). Countries that are considered as powerful place brands tend to enjoy increased inflow of FDIs, tourists, and students (Bose et al., 2016).

Capital inflow, solidified technological base, access to highly skilled labor, and local employment opportunities are some of the potential benefits of the attraction of investments in the city. Jacobsen (2009) created a framework for investor-based place brand equity as the author draws three-place branding functions from an investor's point of view. They are: (a) confidence builder – helps the customer avoid uncertainty and reduces perceived risk of investing and subsequently, transaction costs attached with the investments; (b) symbolic importance – the customer can transfer the place brand identity to their own organization; and (c) provide information – this positions the place in the choice-set of the potential customer.

Jansson and Power (2006) suggests that places having built strong and dynamic brands have an easier task of attracting firms within knowledge industries and proceed to find evidence that strategies to implement place brands are an essential component in the competition of attracting inward investments. When investors choose locations for foreign ventures, they are the buyer and the location (country, region, city) is the product (Papadopoulos, 2004). Consequently, cities promote their best location to attract investors and if the cities promote business areas it will attract businesses and further investors.

There are several factors to take into consideration for building a city target group as they differ from their perceptions of a place and the places' needs and demands. The city customers are usually interested in a suitable environment for their purposes. So, as residents look for an attractive living environment, businesses look for a suitable business environment. The same reasoning applies to visitors as well. If visitors are tourists, they are searching for leisure time activities like shopping malls or cultural offering, while investors, on the other hand, are more interested in business topics, such as business events (i.e., trade fairs) (Sarmento, Farhangmehr, & Simões, 2015), business conventions, and conferences (Mair, 2012).

Destination should be viewed as complex products. As one location cannot be seen separately from other useful locations, the destination offering is not a single location but a package of locations. The product for the tourists and business visitors' overlaps to some extent with the product for the city residents. As Zanker and Braun (2010) compares it to a shopping mall – as an illustrating metaphor – a place offers a large assortment for everybody and each customer fills his or her shopping bag individually.

In this context, BIDs are a major asset in attracting businesses and investors. In fact, BIDs have all the right characteristics for becoming a brand for the city. The main task of urban governance is the creation of urban conditions sufficiently attractive to lure prospective firms, to attract investments, and to safeguard and enhance the city development prospects (Kavaratzis, 2007). BIDs are a low-cost strategy to encourage the private sector to be attractive. Businesses and investors are usually attracted by places that have a certain degree of deregulation and the presence of the government is rationally low, and in this case, BIDs can serve as self-regulated landmarks to attract businesses. The creation of a recognizable place identity requires more than civic consciousness; it requires a clear vision for the place and especially the private sector due to more innovative elements having the ability to successfully accomplish this (Kavaratzis & Ashworth, 2005).

Investment attractiveness is one of the critical dimensions of place branding and acts both as cause and consequence of place branding and thus place brand equity. However, it should be taken into account only to a certain degree. Scholars of place branding tend to consider investment (FDI and domestic) as just a consequence of place branding. Investment attractiveness generally cannot be considered as an established dimension of place brand equity though there is voluminous research in that context in the domains of international business (Bose et al., 2016).

Of significant importance to city marketing and city branding is tourism attractiveness. The perception of the city affects its attractiveness to tourists and foreign investors and also to potential foreign students or local residents. The overall image of the city can be stimulated through a variety of marketing activities. Image capital makes up the unique properties of a destination (Tasci & Gartner, 2007). The effect of brand valuation on destinations would, therefore, be indirect and measured more through changes in the number of tourists who choose the destination, their expenditure levels, and length of stay (Gartner &

Ruzzier, 2011). An underperforming destination brand would expect to receive fewer tourists, with shorter lengths of stay, and lower levels of spending than one that has a strong and positive connection with the market.

2.6 BIDs and Entrepreneurial Urbanism

Entrepreneurial urbanism captures recent changes, addressing the changing form, function, and practices of urban governance (Ward, 2010). Cities shifted their focus to capital accumulation and economic growth (Jessop & Sum, 2000) and promoted the capacities of their respective economic spaces in the face of intensified competition in the global economy (Jessop, 2003).

As manufacturing industry shifted its focus to overseas locations, cities began to move their attention toward encouraging an alternative basis for their development in the new economy, and within the context of deindustrialization and depopulation, the main goal of regeneration is to generate employment, preferably in the form of middle- to high-income jobs in the service sector (Jones & Evans, 2008). While relatively footloose in terms of material resource demands, service industries tend to cluster in areas that provide an attractive living and business environment in order to profit from agglomerate economies (O'Sullivan, 2012). Entrepreneurial urbanism has been referred to within the field of urban studies to broadly capture recent processes of decentralization and the shift from "local government to local governance" (Dobson & Jorgensen, 2014).

In one of the first works on entrepreneurial urbanism, Harvey (1989) outlines the characteristics of this form of local governance: first, as its foundation, entrepreneurial urbanism has the notion of a "public-private partnership", in which a traditional local improvement is integrated with the use of local governmental influences to attract external sources of investment. Second, the activity of the public-private partnership is considered entrepreneurial since it is speculative in design and implementation, followed by all the risks of speculative activities, and opposed to rationally planned and coordinated development. Third, the entrepreneurial urbanism focuses much more closely on the political economy of the place rather than of the territory, since they are designed primarily to improve conditions of living or working within a particular jurisdiction (as it is the case of BIDs).

Building on the work of Harvey (1989), Jessop and Sum (2000) defines main features of entrepreneurial urbanism: first, cities pursue innovative strategies intended to maintain or improve economic competitiveness with other cities or regions; second, strategies are more active and flexible, or pursued in an "entrepreneurial fashion"; third, the city is promoted in an entrepreneurial narrative and marketed as entrepreneurial.

Furthermore, Smitha (2017) explains the entrepreneurial urban process in the framework of a neoliberal project characterized by (1) cities as sources of innovation, competition, and economic growth; (2) a market-based solution to the labor market; (3) promote principles of solidarity and subsidiarity; (4) encourage partnerships and networks to improve infrastructure and increase entrepreneurial competitiveness; (5) decision driven by cost-benefit rather than service, equity, and social welfare.

As we displayed in the previous chapter, in order to attract businesses and visitors' cities seek to establish cultural pursuits, such as theatres, art and shopping facilities, sport and conference facilities, and an attractive living environment. Furthermore, the physically built environment constitutes the other assets that drive economic regeneration, as modern offices for businesses, large-scale infrastructure planning, an effective modern transport system to allow access to attractions and facilities (Jones & Evans, 2008). Another increasingly critical element according to Jones and Evans (2008) is the information communications technology infrastructure, providing access in public spaces, homes, and schools. For example, one of the most successful approaches of entrepreneurial urbanism is smart cities. A smart city is a city performing well in a forward-looking way in economy, people, governance, mobility, environment, and living, built on the smart combination of endowments and activities of self-decisive, independent, and aware citizens (Giffinger et al., 2007), "connecting the physical infrastructure, the IT infrastructure, the social infrastructure, and the business infrastructure to leverage the collective intelligence of the city" (Harrison et al., 2010).

Cities are undergoing transformational projects and initiatives to improve their service to their citizens with the participation and involvement of multiple stakeholders (Giffinger et al., 2007). Thus, several cities have felt an increased need for better governance to manage these projects and initiatives. Projects of smart cities have an impact on the quality of life of citizens and aim to foster more informed, educated, and participatory citizens (Chourabi et al., 2012). Additionally, smart city initiatives allow members of the city to participate in the governance and management of the city and become active users and if they are key players they may have the opportunity to engage with the initiative to the extent that they can influence the project to be a success or a failure (Chourabi et al., 2012).

Jones and Evans (2008) have outlined some economic policies that have supported entrepreneurial urbanism and regeneration as improving the knowledge base, encouraging enterprise, investing in education, training, and empowering local businesses. This also requires an increase in the degree of decentralization, or localism, which requires urban communities and businesses to reduce external economic dependencies through a participatory planning and democratization of space (Dobson & Jorgensen, 2014). The shift from managerial to entrepreneurial forms of governance in many western cities came as a process of globalization and de-industrialization created a need to attract mobile capital and as the service sector took over the national economy, cities became sources of economic growth and experience (Granger, 2010).

Based on the work of Schumpeter on innovation, Jessop & Sum (2000) suggests five possible types of innovative urban forms in the framework of entrepreneurial urbanism:

- The introduction of new types of urban places or spaces for producing, servicing, working, consuming, living, etc. Recent examples include techno poles, intelligent cities, cross-border cities, multicultural cities, and cities organized around integrated transport and sustainable development.
- New methods of space or place production to create location-specific advantages for producing goods/services or other urban activities, including the installation of new physical, social, and cybernetic infrastructures, the promotion of scale and agglomeration economies, regulatory undercutting, or creating new forms of labor market relation.
- Opening new markets – whether by place marketing specific cities in new areas and/or modifying the spatial division of consumption through enhancing the quality of life for residents, commuters, or visitors.
- Finding new sources of supply to enhance competitive advantages. Examples include new sources or patterns of immigration; changing cultural mix of cities; finding new sources of funding from the central state, development agencies, and attracting inward investment or reskilling the workforce.
- Refiguring or redefining the urban hierarchy and/or altering the place of a given city within it. Examples include the development of a world or global city position, regional gateways, hubs, cross-border regions, and "virtual regions" based on interregional cooperation.

Urban entrepreneurialism brought BIDs as a policy tool to change the business structure of a city and to provide more independence to them. Considering the work of Jessop and Sum (2000) BIDs can be included in the introduction of new types of urban spaces for producing, servicing, working, consuming, and living. Because the authors take a general approach to the entrepreneurial urbanism, they do not particularly mention BIDs. However, the characteristics of the "urban spaces" they refer to are the same as those of the BIDs. The standard policy tool change in urban entrepreneurialism has four components, as explained by Ward (2010): (1) an institutional blueprint, as in the governance arrangements in terms of the board structure and the nature of those parties involved; (2) the relationship of the BID to other institutions involved in aspects of urban security and maintenance; (3) the range and type of strategies used by the BID; and (4) the use of key performance indicators to audit and evaluate the performance of the BID.

In the context of tourism development, entrepreneurial cities can approach two policies suggested by Ward (2012): on the one hand, *event-led policy tourism*. Policy actors of various stripes are invited to share their experiences, to speak about their involvement in their own city's redevelopment strategies. Urban managers will spell out the details of their city's success stories, pointing to examples of how areas have been redeveloped. Professionals such as architects, economists, engineers, designers, and planners will bring their specific, technical knowledge to the table, sharing examples of cases in which they have been involved. On the other hand, *visit-led policy tourism* involves visiting and touring cities that have become known for their successful approaches. Groups of policy actors from one city visit another city to see and to learn from its own policy actors about "the processes, challenges, and benefits of the formulation and realization of particular policy models".

In the context of investment, the policy rationale of the entrepreneurial urbanism is directed toward the concept of regional competition: cities create a stimulating environment by structuring institutions and regulations in order to help inner firms to produce and grow. On the other hand, cities invest in infrastructure; promote their economic structure, their location, and their governance as well as urban strategy to attract outside firms to position in the city, to invest and to create jobs (Malecki, 2004). Much of the work of the entrepreneurial urbanism in the regional competition for businesses and investors is actually focused on city marketing (Graham, 2002), as one of the most influential determinants remains the general perception of the city (Jacobsen, 2009), and therefore cities promote their best location to attract investors (as it is the case for the tourist as well; Papadopoulos [2004]).

2.7 BIDs Role in Supporting SMEs

Policymakers have been increasingly interested in how businesses start-up and grow. Small- and medium-sized enterprises have been important drivers of economic growth. Businesses create two-thirds of all new jobs and more than two-thirds of the innovation in the economy and have accounted for two-thirds of the differences in economic growth rates among industrialized nations (Walburn, 2005). On the other hand some of the most successful BIDs in the United States are local and homogeneous and occupy relatively small places in an urban area, thereby ensuring stakeholders within the district have common goals and concerns, important for collective action and effective collaboration (Hogg, Medway, & Warnaby, 2003).

The existence of BIDs or BID-like structures is an important factor for the performance of small businesses. The United States has also implemented programs which include only a small number of SMEs in the BIDs or like Stokes (2006) describes the micro district programs as built on the notion that smaller business areas are not as organized as larger business districts and therefore are not able to take advantage of efforts to collectivize resources and perform revitalization projects. Micro business districts provide organized and targeted assistance in areas such as business development and retention, marketing, organization, funding, and special events, designed to serve business districts that have an insufficient number of businesses to form a BID (Stokes, 2007).

According to Hogg et al. (2003) there are some key advantages for SMEs entering BIDs:

- BID activities are designed specifically to address the local needs of the paying stakeholders, as the improvement of the visual appearance of the areas, services like transport, employment schemes, and local training. BIDs can promote the identity of the area to both internal and external audiences.
- Collective action strengthens the demands of SMEs and increases the ability to influence local government policy relating to their specific area.
- The network of support for SMEs could benefit from the experiences of others in the BID, forging stronger local links between businesses.

Several of the services mentioned can be more beneficial to SMEs rather than big enterprises. These services include marketing, policy advocacy, capital improvements, and strategic planning (Mitchell, 2008).

Owner-managers of SMEs may be expected to be fully aware of the product or service markets that their business is based in, but they may not be trained or proficient in accounting or financial management (Marriott & Marriott, 2000). Hence, they may turn to advisers, especially external accountants, for financial management advice and perhaps wider assistance. Business advisers have interests, either for commercial or government initiative reasons, to "sell" new ideas to SME owner-managers for use in their businesses. External advisers, especially its bankers and external accountants, who have a unique relationship with a business, may also be mentors to owner-managers in general management, planning, and control issues, including cost management. (Berry, Sweeting, & Goto, 2006).

In the cases of BID external advising is part of the strategic planning, which makes it easier for the businesses both to access an adviser and to reduce the costs of advising. SMEs need to set long-term organizational goals, develop and implement plans to achieve these goals, while planning the use of their resources in order for them to use their competitive advantage to gain as much efficiency as possible (Wang, Walker, & Redmond, 2007). Moreover, SMEs that engage in strategic planning are also more likely to be those enterprises that are more innovative, that have more newly patented products, that employ new process and management technologies, and that achieve international growth (Gibbons & O'Connor, 2005). Perhaps most importantly, SMEs that engage in strategic planning are less likely to be those that fail (Wang et al., 2007).

Furthermore, there are networking factors that influence the performance of the SMEs, and more specifically, innovation. The importance of BIDs relies also on the creation of social capital within the district by compromising norms and networks of trust and reciprocity (Lloyd et al., 2003). As previously explained, these theories suggest that from investing in social capital, or in social relations with expected returns, the benefits belong to the whole group that takes part in these social relations (Lin, 2017).

The institutional structure of BIDs is appropriate for accelerating social capital by means of networking, cooperation for the common goals, and building trust through continuous relations (Lloyd et al., 2003). Cooke and Wills (1999) have long-established an important relationship between social capital, SMEs, and their performance, mainly through the channel of innovation. According to the authors, what is of particular importance to this process is the promotion of linkage to networks, the existence of synergy whereby SMEs have close links to program executives, and the formation of integration by embedding firms more firmly in indigenous SME networks.

The literature on the factors that restrict and facilitate SME innovation suggests that SMEs tend to face higher barriers to innovation than their larger counterpart (Nieto & Santamaria, 2010). Studies have highlighted a broad range of factors that act as barriers to SME innovation, including factors internal, for instance, financial issues, marketing skills, strategic planning, management, and personal characteristic and external, for instance, demand, supply, and environmental issues to the firm (Hall, Lotti, & Mairesse, 2009).

SMEs may overcome such barriers through a range of external environmental, structural and firm-specific characteristics that have been identified as contributing to affecting SME innovation and success which include, networking, regional support, business planning and strategy, and entrepreneurial characteristics (Laforet, 2011). Quinn, McKitterick, McAdam, and Brennan (2013) emphasize the importance of networks for innovation, whereas organizations interact and exchange ideas, knowledge, and resources with actors such as customers, suppliers, public and private research institutions, and employees within their internal environment. This can help small firms overcome skills shortage that would otherwise limit their ability to innovate.

One of the most provided services by BIDs is the consumers marketing (Hoyt, 2005a; Mitchell, 2001). As it was previously discussed through aggressive marketing campaigns and other forms of self-promotion, BIDs effectively attract visitors and investors. O'Dwyer, Gilmore, and Carson (2009) highlight the primary role of the owner-manager in the SME marketing, a generalist who has to have a vision of where the business is going and at the same time to take care of the operational details carried out in the firm, greatly influenced by the decision-making. The authors argue that marketing is often misunderstood and underutilized by owner-managers and may define marketing as quite narrowly relating only to selling and promoting, but the actual marketing done may still cover a wide range of marketing practices. For the SMEs, it is easier to take part in an effective marketing campaign as they are directed by the BIDs authorities and not by their owner-manager.

BIDs usually adapt a joint marketing initiative, which is constructed around both consumers and destination marketing. BIDs brand marketing campaigns create a homogeneous marketable image that, coupled with capital improvement create a general image of the area (Hogg, Medway, & Warnaby, 2004). SMEs profit from the general image, or the brand of the BID in the same way firms within the city profit from the general image of the city. This creates a perception of the BIDs identity and the conditions and characteristics accompanying it (Kavaratzis, 2007).

2.8 Policy Transfer

BIDs have proved to be a compelling international model (Briffault, 1999; Morçöl & Wolf, 2010; Peel et al., 2009). Policy transfer is a term that describes the voluntary flow of ideas between individuals and is regarded as a type of policy learning because it involves the acquisition and utilization of knowledge about policies elsewhere or in other words, policy transfer attends to the way that policies and practices in one context are used to develop policies and practices in other settings (Dolowitz & Marsh, 2000).

Mossberger and Wolman (2003) suggest a potential value in learning from the experience of others in policy-making by assessing similarities of problems and goals, their policy performance, and differences in settings. Learning through policy transfer can minimize any potential mistakes and realize additional efficiency gains, which is a significant development in public-sector policy and practice (Peel & Lloyd, 2005a). Furthermore, there should be a more robust understanding of relevant conditions, policy, and the institutional environment when considering the potential transfer of policies and programs (Mossberger & Wolman, 2003).

Peel and Lloyd (2005b) highlight the importance of understanding the relevant exporting and importing conditions when considering the transfer potential of particular policies and programs, the problems that may arise when policies and programs are uncritically transferred from one context to another. It is argued that it is critical that political and economic contextual circumstances be taken into account when considering the transfer of policy mechanisms and instruments (Dassler & Parker, 2004).

The transfer of urban policy is an increasingly common practice because public sector involvement and support for revitalization efforts are diminishing, thus, new coping mechanisms are necessary. Advancements in information and communication technologies, like the Internet, allow urban policy entrepreneurs to save time and resources in importing best practices from other cities (Hoyt, 2008). Such quick importations of practices are a cause for concern because some policy entrepreneurs adopt new concepts without critically analyzing the legislative, economic, political, and other differences between the exporting and importing contexts (Mossberger & Wolman, 2003). This hurried new policy importation may fail to solve the urban problems it was intended to resolve or may even aggravate them. Despite the widespread use of the model, many BID advocates have been unable to import the tool into their own districts because of certain place-based characteristics that make this transfer difficult (Rothrock, 2008).

The case of policy transfer essentially considers appropriate and successful policies, and in order to fully understand the policy transfer of BIDs a conceptual framework needs to address not only the procedural nature of policy, but also the social construction of success and appropriateness (Cook, 2008). On one hand, urban policy mobility involves the circulation of ideas, techniques, and practices among several places, and on the other hand, they involve the production of new sets of relations and networks at local and inter-local levels (Crivello, 2015). Cook (2008) suggests a framework of six core aspects of policy transfer:

1 The identification and construction of domestic policy problems
2 How policies are strategically selected and interpreted as being successful and appropriate
3 How models are re-embedded into and reshaped in the new context
4 How and why actually existing policies are broadly used as a legitimization tool
5 The actors and institutions involved in the policy transfer process and their roles within this
6 The exclusions and silences within the policy transfer process (how existing policies and practices are excluded or involved in policy transfer)

In the context of the BIDs, as it was previously explained, Ward (2010) explains the policy transfer tool in four components: (1) an institutional blueprint; (2) the relationship of the BID to other institutions involved in aspects of urban security and maintenance; (3) the range and type of strategies used by the BID; and (4) the use of key performance indicators to audit and evaluate the performance of the BID.

BID model has been transferred from one locality to another, within and across national borders. The first policy transfer of BIDs was the transfer from Canada to the United States in the 1970s, but it is unclear how the policy transfer happened (Hoyt, 2008). Nevertheless, what is studied as a successful policy transfer of BIDs, is the case of transfer from the United States to the UK, which was conducted by a state-sponsored economic development network of different geographical focus and reaches, including different sorts of practitioners, such as architectures, engineers, and planners (Jonas & Wood, 2016). In some cases, the BID model has been moved through existing networks, such as those organized more broadly around local economic development, and in other cases, specific networks have been established around the city center and downtown revitalization (Jonas & Wood, 2016).

After careful and extensive research and a long debate, the first BID was implemented in 2004 and began operations in 2005 (Hoyt, 2008). But the investigation into the adoption of the BID model began in 1992 by studying organizations in the United States, and several public sector bodies and national businesses provided the funding and support for a pilot BID project a decade later (Symes & Steel, 2003). The 1990s witnessed the widespread introduction of formal and informal local public-private partnerships (PPPs) responsible for the management of town and city centers in the UK, known as town center management schemes, operating a mixture of "janitorial" public space maintenance and more strategic planning and promotion of their centers but the BID model implemented in the United States became more attractive due to its performance there (Cook, 2008).

The British government looked at the experience in the United States with BIDs and decided to change the legislation so that the American model could be imported and implemented in the United Kingdom (Lloyd et al., 2003). In particular, the experiences of a handful of New York's and Philadelphia's BIDs formed the empirical evidence on which the government of the UK was convinced of both the policy's "local" successes and its ability to enhance urban entrepreneurialism (Ward, 2007). The pilot wave of BIDs tested the strategy in different locations by a well-defined policy action (Tallon, 2013):

- Establishing a required level and nature of managerial skills and capability
- Producing reliable guidance on operational, training, and recruitment issues
- Identifying resources, timescales, mechanisms, and capacities
- Testing and validating the role of the partner agencies involved
- Producing a good practice document and an information database
- Defining the process
- Validate guidance and inform secondary legislation

2.9 Assessing BIDs Performance

In previous sections, while addressing accountability issues of the BIDs we identified three major stakeholders (Hochleutner, 2003):

1 the local property or business owners subject to BID assessments (Owners);
2 residents of the BID (BID Residents); and
3 residents of the municipality (City Residents).

Indirect stakeholders are those who receive residual benefits from BIDs, such as customers, visitors, local institutions, and residents adjacent to a BID, parties which may be affected by the BID's activities although they may not pay directly for the services (if the tax is not passed on to them in the form of higher prices) or be targeted by the programs and services (Caruso & Weber, 2008). Furthermore, we mentioned that in order to assess BID activity, there is a need to implement and monitor performance indicators in compliance with their nature and mission (Hoyt & Gopal-Agge, 2007). The idea of performance related to outcomes represents a shift from the traditional monitoring compliance in terms of inputs and process standards, toward program efficiency in terms of public benefits (Caruso & Weber, 2008).

A good program accounts for both the inputs of the program and the outputs and outcomes: inputs are the resources used in delivering the various services, while outputs are measurable units of services that are delivered within a specified period, and outcomes are the benefits that the stakeholders realize from the services (Hatry, 1999). Therefore, performance measurements are needed to evaluate a program. Performance measurement refers to the collection of data on key performance indicators in order to manage this performance or to strategically use performance information to correct problems before they manifest in performance deficiencies (Poister, 2003).

While in the private sector the performance measurement systems are relatively advanced and effective, the issues arise in the public sector. There is a wider range of critical stakeholders, often with conflicting interests and each able to exert a significant impact on the public sphere, and in addition, the finances of the public sector are significantly different (Jarrar & Schiuma, 2007). Even more difficult is measuring the performance of the hybrid organizations, or public-private partnerships as well as quasi-governmental institutions as exercising accountability in PPPs ultimately depends on clarifying responsibilities in relationships (Forrer, Kee, Newcomer, & Boyer, 2010).

Organizations use different means of attributing results to program inputs, although few undertake the statistical analysis necessary to demonstrate more robust causality. Outcomes may include both intermediate program measures and wider societal measures (Poister, 2003). The most common goals of performance measurement and management are to reduce costs (increase efficiency), increase effectiveness (or cost-effectiveness), maintain equity, and deliver high-quality products that are met with high levels of customer satisfaction; at a deeper level, the purposes may include accountability to citizens, justifying increased resources, and political and popular support. Among others; deeper still, the goal may be to remain competitive with benchmark cities, attract residents and businesses, and portray the image of a progressive community with a high quality of life.

Mitchell (2008) structures a framework for the evaluation of the BIDs performance in four categories:

1 *Diligence* (the enumeration of tasks performed): This is the first and most basic level of evaluating BIDs. In the process of implementing projects, BIDs must make sure that goals are specified, funded, monitored, and completed. The most effective way to do this is by making goals tangible, and all that has to be done is keeping track of daily tasks.
2 *Effectiveness* (the achievement of tangible impacts): The level of activities is not a sufficient indicator for the success of the BIDs. BIDs measure the effectiveness of their activities by identifying outcomes within the areas they control. Both qualitative and quantitative data are required for proper evaluation. Data may vary from business openings and closings, unemployment rates, crime rates, lease rates, occupancy rates, taxable retail sales, business license revenues, residential housing sales, and hosting capabilities. The difficulty with the measurement of factual outcomes is the inability to isolate the effects of BIDs as there may be multiple factors determining the outcomes.
3 *Responsiveness*: Business response is the measure of whether businesses wish to renew the BID. But, the evaluation must not be limited simply to the renewal vote and a more analytical view of the progress and achievements are not taken into consideration. Usually good practices of evaluation of responsiveness include surveys and anecdotes. Surveys can be conducted to businesses, residents, visitors, shoppers, and workers, about their opinions and views of city places and the performance of the BID. Anecdotes include the production of newsletters and reports completed

with quotes, personal stories, and case studies in order to assess the work of BIDs.

4 *Sociability* (the contribution to city life): Sociability is evaluated by measuring the influence of BIDs on the culture of cities. The focus is on the fairness of BIDs toward different people the extent to which BIDs are democratically accountable, and the ways BIDs shape the character of cities. No methodology is involved in the examination of sociability but rather the basis for accepting any conclusion is the logical quality of the argument. In contrast to the proceeding evaluations of BIDs, the assessment of sociability has come more often from sources outside of BIDs.

The evaluation structure of Mitchell (2008) is more of a general nature. Caruso and Weber (2008) identified some more specific and tangible performance measures for the BIDs:

1 *Real Estate Development*: The effectiveness of a BID as a real estate development tool can be judged by its ability to influence the value of properties inside the district. Achieving the other goals of eliminating development obstacles (such as a lack of available parking) and improving an area's appearance as well as investing in infrastructure and services within BID districts could improve the quality and magnitude of products and services consumed there. If businesses are more profitable or residents feel more secure in the district, demand for the property should increase.

2 *Business Development*: Some measures focus on the internal workings of the businesses represented in the district as opposed to the spaces they occupy, as BIDs aim to enhance the success of businesses operating in the district and attract other businesses to expand. Consequently, some typical measures include the number of businesses in the area, taxable sales, and employment figures.

3 *Convenience*: Accessibility can draw people to the district and a perception of lack of accessibility can repel potential customers who do not wish to navigate the streets and parking lots. Therefore, outputs may include additional traffic-calming devices, off- and on-street parking, loading zones, shared car programs, bus lanes, bicycle racks, transit stations, and pedestrian crossing locations. In accordance with each output, data can be easily collected, analyzed, and compared to other BIDs.

4 *Identity*: BIDs attempt to compete by promoting a distinctive identity that can justify the additional trouble of getting there or the slightly higher prices of small, locally owned stores. BIDs

promote themselves to customers and visitors through special events, advertising campaigns, district directories, websites, and media coverage. Thus, outputs may include enhanced name recognition, media coverage, distribution numbers of published business directories, website visit counts, and sale increases during a promotional event, etc.

5   *Attractiveness*: One of the BIDs goals is to improve their internal environment. These public works include elements in the streetscape such as sidewalks, light poles, banners, hanging baskets, street furniture, landscaping, and decorative structures. The public way can also include streets and landscape medians, malls and plazas, parks, and other spaces open to the public. Nevertheless, performance indicators for the aesthetic quality of the public way are difficult to track because no third party collects relevant information in a manner similar to a municipality collecting sales taxes or employment figures.

6   *Safety*: Statistics on crimes committed in BIDs can be kept by the municipal police departments as well as security firms contracted through the BID service provider. The number of reported crimes, arrests, interventions, or assistance provided by security officers could be collected on a regular basis. If possible, data prior to a BID security program should be compared to the period after which the BID security program is in place to observe the possibility of a correlation between crime rates and BID security programs.

Overall, we can see that some of the performance measures are easily recognizable and tangible in nature, such as improved sidewalks, landscaping, better maintenance of various public areas, improved lighting of a parking facility, and new way-finding signage are all visible indicators that have been used to improve a particular aspect of the commercial district. Some other performance measures are more difficult to collect and to analyze, but there are several techniques that can accomplish robust results. In a more precise performance assessment, performance indicators need to be established, so when measures take place, the values can be compared to the standard value, target value, or benchmark (Lehtonen, 2015).

3   A Short Analysis of the Different Models of BIDs

3.1 City Improvement Districts

The transfer of the concept of BIDs under the name "CIDs" started in the early 1990s in Johannesburg. It has since spread widely to other cities such as Pretoria and Cape Town with the private sector playing a key role in the transfer of the model by adopting the legislation and the spread of CIDs within the city (Peyroux, 2008). Indeed, CIDs were introduced by the private sector in the early 1990s in response to the concern within the private and public sectors over economic and business decline in city centers, fall in property values, and tax base (Didier, Morange, & Peyroux, 2013).

The city was largely impacted by the rise of suburban economic nodes from the 1970s onward. The relocation of department stores in the 1980s and the capital flight in the 1990s, as the office vacancies increased, led to rents decreasing and property values sunk while large companies relocated to the northern suburbs (Beavon, 2004). In Johannesburg, members of private sector felt a strong perception on the loss of control over the environment. They introduced CIDs to make up for the failure of public authorities to deliver appropriate standards of service (Didier et al., 2013).

The long-established Central Johannesburg Partnership organized study tours of US BIDs with regional and city officers in the mid-1990s aimed at visiting CID sites and learn from international experiences in order to set up practices and legislation for a CID in Johannesburg. This marked the beginning of lobbying for the establishment of the first CID as early as 1993, and subsequently was part of the drafting of the CID legislation later on (Peyroux, 2008). The pilot project which was focused on "crime and grime" proved to be a success and several CIDs were established afterward. The capacity of CJP to convince the local owners and businesses played an essential role in the success of the model. This was because the delegation of some daily management issues proved to be a relief for the municipality (Didier et al., 2013). Furthermore, the support from the municipality was central to the success of the policy transfer. In 2001 the municipality created the Johannesburg Development Agency and also involved the CIDs in the framework, thus co-financing some of them (Peyroux, 2006).

In terms of governance, while most of the CIDs of Johannesburg's inner city are managed by the CJP, public involvement is important as the cities municipality has integrated CIDs into the 2004 "Inner City Regeneration Strategy Business Plan" and uses the additional provision of services, as well as marketing and branding activities to develop special zones (Didier et al., 2013): (1) the cultural zone of Newtown; (2) the Fashion District; (3) the heritage tourism district of Constitution Hill; (4) Ellis Park; (4) a sports zone developed for the 2010 World Cup (Didier et al., 2013).

According to the latest assessment of the CID (City Improvement District Forum, 2016), the following are some of the characteristics:

- 18 legislated CIDs in Johannesburg.
- CIDs occupy a 7.6-km footprint within the City of Johannesburg.
- 18 CIDs have been legislated between 1998 and 2013.
- 1,828 properties and 1,099 property owners.
- Total estimated municipal value of CID properties is $4.73 billion, and $6 billion for both legislated and voluntary CIDs.
- Offices represent 58.8% of land use within the CIDs boundaries and residential is 16.4%.
- A combined total of 715 jobs are maintained monthly.
- The annual budget of the CIDs is more than $6.2 million, this is displayed in the main services supplied.
  - Security – 56%
  - Cleaning – 19%
  - Place making & marketing – 3%
  - Infrastructure upgrades – 1%
  - General CID administration – 14%
  - Other & Special projects – 7%

The report also highlights some qualitative improvements in the CID area:

- The support for the local economy.
- Contribution to social investment initiatives.
- CIDs are responsible for the creation of both direct and indirect jobs and employment in industries including management

companies, legal, auditing, cleaning, security, and landscaping; the report estimates 20,000 indirect jobs within the inner city.

* The structure of CIDs allows for the development and management of large events.
* CIDs contribute to the creation and management of destinations that attract local and international tourism.
* CIDs actively contribute to improving neighborhood perceptions through well-managed urban spaces.
* Improved quality of life in CID areas results in the increase of the city's property tax base.

Overall the social inflection of the CID model is driven by a private stakeholder, a housing company that has large assets in the inner city. Safety is in the core of the CIDs in the inner city, as it has become a key driver for investment in a relatively turbulent city, while general administration is also highlighted. Promoting social capital and trust among the communities, in particular between tenants and landlords, represents an attempt to support capital investment by allegedly addressing social development, an evolution which has been supported by public policies in a context of political stability and continuity at local level (Didier et al., 2013).

3.2 BIAs

A Business Improvement Area (BIA) is a "made-in-Ontario" innovation that allows local business people and commercial property owners and tenants to join together. With the support of the municipality, they organize, finance, carry out physical improvements, and promote economic development in their district (Government of Ontario, 2010). BIDs have originated in Canada, and the BIA has no significant difference with the BID, while the BIAs (or BIDs) in Canada have a higher participation level of the local government, probably the highest participation of the BIDs model (Mitchell, 2008). The municipality of Ontario frequently publishes a document, *Ontario BIA Handbook*, where a summary of BIAs progress in multiple areas is laid out. According to the latest by date of this handbook (Government of Ontario, 2010) there were more than 230 BIAs in place across the province varying in size from less than 60 businesses and property owners to more than 2,000, with a large list of services:

* *Capital Improvements*: Streetscape projects, such as installing pedestrian-scale lighting and street furniture, planting trees and

shrubbery, sidewalk treatment, facade improvements, and other urban design.

- *Consumer Marketing*: Producing and promoting festivals and events, setting out seasonal decorations to create a pleasant environment, coordinating sales promotions, producing maps and newsletters, adding signage and banners, launching image enhancement, and advertising campaigns.

- *Economic Development*: Offering incentives (such as loans) to new and expanding businesses, working with property owners to ensure that all available space is occupied and that a desirable business and service mix is maintained, conducting market research, producing data-oriented reports, marketing to investors, enhancing community educational facilities, and engaging in transit and land-use planning efforts.

- *Maintenance*: Collecting waste, removing litter and graffiti, washing sidewalks, trimming trees, cutting grass, cleaning footpaths, and maintaining flowerbeds.

- *Parking and Transportation*: Managing public parking systems, maintaining transit shelters.

- *Policy Advocacy*: Promoting public policies to the community, lobbying government on behalf of business interests.

- *Public Space Regulation*: Managing sidewalk vending and street performances, discouraging panhandling, controlling vehicle loading and unloading, enforcing by-law compliance.

- *Security*: Providing supplementary security guards and street guides, buying and installing electronic security systems, working with the local police force.

- *Social Services*: Aiding the homeless, providing job training, supplying youth services, hiring at a decent wage formerly homeless individuals, or those making the transfer from welfare to work.

The structure in assistance of the BIAs is The Ontario BIA Association which represents BIAs across Ontario, also supports and advocates on behalf of its members. The association has built strong performance indicator and publishes an annual report which evaluates the performance of the BIAs in the area (The Ontario BIAs Association, 2017):

3.2.1 Street Appeal

- Streetscape and Façade Investment: 55% of reporting BIAs had members leveraging façade programs, which generated an average 2.5:1 private sector to municipality investment ratio with an average of $0.17 per capita invested.

- Place making:
  - BIAs report a median spend of $32,500 annually dedicated to beautification.
  - 75% have a significant stock of properties that are either heritage-designated or of heritage interest.
  - All BIAs reported having multiple transit stops.

3.2.2 Economic Development

- Employment:
  - The project team found both BIAs that can attract employees to an area increasing the daytime population by over 800% and BIAs that account for a significant proportion of the jobs in a community (ranging from 0.2:1 to 0.9:1).
  - The greatest average daytime employment shifts (the increase from residential population to daytime employment population) occur in BIAs in municipalities with a population of 100,000–500,000, where the average shift is a 177% increase.
- Building Permits: From 2011 to 2016, the value of building permits in reporting communities increased by 163% (commercial) and 128% (residential), while the number of permits remained relatively stable.
- New Business Openings: An average of 6% of their membership represents new businesses.
- Assessed Property Value (Average): Assessed value was $216 million. In communities with a population between 100,000 and 500,000, this value was 25% higher than the average, whereas in communities between 500,000 and 1M in population, the value was 125% below average.

3.2.3 Support Local Business

- Vacancy: On average, there were 11.7 vacancies per BIA on an annual basis. This figure is significantly higher in communities with a population of 100,000–500,000 population, having an average of 21.6 vacancies per year.
- Number of chains: On average, chains make up 7% of BIA membership in Ontario, with cities 100,000–500,000 in population reaching as high as 12%.
- Things to do within the area of influence of a BIA: On average a BIA has ten places of worship, 12 public parks, and two cultural facilities within 500 m of the BIA, making them prime civic spaces for public engagement.

3.2.4 Community Building

- Strategic Plan Achievement: 40% of BIAs review their strategic plan annually and that 76% review their plan within one to five years.
- Municipal Capacity Building:
  - 84% of BIA staff rate their level of collaboration with their municipal partners between 7 and ten (ten being excellent).
  - While 97% report having a relationship with municipal staff; they only rate the effectiveness of these relationships at 81%.
- Local Capacity Building: BIAs produce an estimated total of 1,200 events. Each year, an additional 1,300 produced by other community organizations land within the BIA.
- Safe Environment:
  - Of the BIAs surveyed, 60% have at least one policing center within 500 m
  - 30% of crime within a BIA was theft and shoplifting, 24% was alcohol or quality of life related, and 14% was considered violent crime.

As it is expected from a well-established BIA association, the report constitutes in well-defined performance indicators and measures. These performance indicators and key statistics are both easily recognizable and tangible, both relevant to the local property or business owners, residents of the BID, and residents of the municipality. The report is focused on the overall performance of the BIAs and the supply of services has a wide focus.

A key characteristic of the BIAs is the involvement of the municipality in their operations. Members of the municipality are usually part of the board of the directors and they actively take part in the decisions of the BIAs. Some of the main involvements include (Government of Ontario, 2010):

- Staff assistance to business leaders in organizing meetings and promotion in the initial conceptualization stages
- Council approval is required to establish a BIA
- Public consultation process – petition/objections
- Council representative on the board of management
- Approval of annual budget and financial monitoring

3.3 DIDs

In 1999, the Japanese government passed legislation allowing the creation of Town Management Organizations (TMOs) to assist with the revitalization of downtown improvement districts (DID), the Japanese equivalent of BIDs, or BID-like in that they represent a joint effort between local government and business owners (Hoyt, 2005b).

One characteristic of these policies in Japan is that the central government played a key role. Unlike in the United States where federalism is adopted, the government has been centralized in Japan, and the central government has much more power than local governments and as a result, policies for downtown revitalization are developed mainly by the central government, and local governments only implement policies that the central government establishes (Miyazawa, 2006). Local governments formulate the Basic Plan, which describes proposed development projects and may also specify the need for a TMO and often the city appoints the Chamber of Commerce as the TMO but may select other types of organizations (Hoyt, 2005a).

The TMO model, as with the BID model, copies the centralized management of shopping malls which typically locate in suburb areas and threaten the prosperity of downtown areas. It is often said that one big reason why shopping malls prosper whereas downtowns decline is the difference in the management system between shopping malls and downtowns. That is, the owners of shopping malls can increase the attractiveness of the malls by coordinating tenant selection, promotion, and market research, as well as providing comfortable infrastructure services (Miyazawa, 2006).

According to the study of Miyazawa (2006) 62% of the TMOs offer business recruitment; 43% hold consulting seminars for businesses; 80% of them hold events; 30% make capital improvements to the area; 28% implement market research and 43% implement marketing campaign; and less than 25% offer services such as cleaning, parking, and only 5% offer security services. According to the study more than half of the services are subsidized by the government.

"Marunouchi" is the biggest business district in the Tokyo urban area. In response to a context of economic crisis and deflation promised for decades to come, a new law was passed in 2002 with the aim of boosting the renewal of business districts – the Urban Renaissance Special Measure Law, based on the idea of special zoning, resulting in Urban Renaissance Urgent Development Areas and zones that were even more attractive to the private sector known as Special Urban Renaissance Urgent Development Areas, including Marunouchi (Languillon-Aussel, 2014).

The main investor of the district is Mitsubishi Estate Group. Covering a total area of 1.2 square km, it is home to some 4,000 businesses with a combined worth of around €1 trillion, or over 20% of Japan's gross domestic product, 92 of which are listed in the Tokyo Stock Exchange, and accommodating over 230,000 workers in the district (Mitsubishi Estate Co., 2016). As a result of this urban renaissance project, bringing together private companies and public bodies, "Marunouchi" has experienced a profound transformation of its urban fabric and become more attractive, nevertheless, the renaissance of "Marunouchi" also presents a certain number of limiting factors, not least of which has been the emergence of an oversupply of office space, leading to a recent rise in vacancy rates, although vacancy rates in "Marunouchi" remain lower than in Tokyo's other vice centers (Languillon-Aussel, 2014).

The annual report of the "Marunouchi" business district (Mitsubishi Estate Co., 2016) is actually a report delivered to the businesses in the area, reporting revenues, expenses, urban planning strategies, managing strategies, etc. The main purpose of the area is to provide office space, thus, the main stakeholders are clearly business tenants. Furthermore, the urban planning and the services provided within the area, as in any other TMO, are partially subsidized by the government (Languillon-Aussel, 2014).

3.4 Main Street Associations

Together with the BIDs approach, another approach known as the Main Street Associations (MSAs) or Main Street Programs, or simply Main Street, was developed in the 1970s. As BIDs were designed to improve public services privately in large business areas, work was also done to address the economic decline and associated threats to *small, historic downtowns* and, in 1977, a demonstration "Main Street" program was launched in three Midwestern cities (Ryberg-Webster & Kinahan, 2014). Initiated by the National Trust for Historic Preservation, MSAs had the vision to preserve the existing economic environment through a plan of development which would include also the private sector (Robertson, 2004):

- Organization: fundraising; committee structure; membership recruitment; consensus building and cooperation amongst the many businesses, individuals, institutions, and government offices with a stake in downtown
- Design: enhancement of downtown's physical assets and visual qualities (i.e., buildings, streetscapes, open spaces, waterfronts)
- Promotion: marketing the downtown to the public, working to enhance its image, and hosting events and activities to bring people downtown

- Economic Restructuring: strengthening and diversifying the downtown's economic base

The economic rationale of preservation in contemporary urban planning and revitalization focuses on the place value of historic environments, downtown revitalization, heritage tourism, and local power and politics (Ryberg-Webster & Kinahan, 2014). In other words, the preservation of urban areas is not only to empower local businesses and increase their profitability, but also even more so to preserve the local identity of the area. A more profound reason to the creation of the MSAs is the enhancement of the sense of community, which as Farahani and Lozanovska (2014) describe can be enhanced through the "use of public space factors": (1) the individual factors which are related to the public space; (2) the social factors which are related to the public space; and (3) the physical/environmental factors. This being considered, MSAs tend to improve the physical and environmental factors to create a sense of community and further enhance it by preserving the historical content.

The Texas Main Street Program was established in 1981. Between 1981 and 2001 it has served 136 communities, which included cities with small downtowns with estimated population 1,747, to large city downtown or neighborhood districts such as Houston with a population of over 2 million (Sullivan, Huang, & Abrams, 2006). In the 2006 extended study of the Texas Main Street Program, Sullivan et al. (2006) provided a questionnaire for the managers of the MSAs and provided some key statistics regarding the four-point approach components. The respondents (managers) were asked to rank design, promotion, organization, and economic restructuring based on their impacts on the revitalization of the respondents Main Street District: Design was mentioned as the most important factor by 39%; followed by organization with 23%, promotion with 20%, and economic restructuring mentioned by 18% of the managers.

As in the previous case studies, the MSAs commission, "Texas Main Street Program", provides an annual report on the activities and programs. According to the 2017 report (Drescher, 2018):

- Texas has 89 designated Main Street communities ranging from the very small, with just a few 1000 in population, to urban areas across the state.
- During 2017, more than $500 million was reinvested into Texas' Main Street districts, of which about half came from private investment.

- At year-end, cumulative economic impact figures for communities that are current participants in the program showed more than $3.2 billion in combined public and private reinvestment.
- The Texas Main Street Program:
    - Provided at no cost to designated Main Street programs and their downtown property/business owners, almost 4,300 hours of assistance on specific projects requested by the local;
    - Conducted 161 site visits;
    - Consultations done by the TMSP design staff resulted in more than $10 million in reinvestment.

The report is brief and this seems to be the case even for the previous reports, even though in the 2015 report there are several other indicators mentioned, such as the average annual jobs created, labor income, state and local taxes, and even more details on the stats provided above by the 2017 report stats for the MSAs (Drescher, 2016). As the Texas Main Street Program is funded by the National Trust for Historic Preservation, it receives federal funds, which are then channeled to the projects in the area.

3.5 Lessons Learned

In South Africa, the City Improvement Districts are formed in response to increasing criminal activity, homelessness, problems with informal traders, and a dramatic decline in cleanliness in the area, with the following objectives:

- To combat crime and grime.
- To coordinate revitalization efforts.
- The rapid decline of services to the area required the private sector to partner with the public sector to provide security and cleansing services.

In contrast to the typical BIDs, CIDs in South Africa are more focused on security (as it is more of a concern), than to other business services, as it has proved effective in improving the business environment within the area. Furthermore, there are some services focused in the general administration of the area, which still remain at a basic level.

In Canada, initially, BIAs were formed to promote and maintain the property and businesses that make up the downtown core. Now, BIAs are more involved in producing events and bringing more people into downtown as opposed to beautification and street fixtures pursuing main street revitalization through economic based incentives to developers in order to create high residential densities which in turn supports the businesses of the street. The range of services is wide and proportional, with no particular focus, as the structures value both promotion and the real improvements in the area. There are little or no changes to the BID concept, but there is a more profound role of the local governance in their management, as the municipality is more active in the decision making of the BIAs in contrast to BIDs in the United States.

In Japan, in order to cope with the problem of deterioration in the Downtown Improvement Districts, the city formed the Basic Plan, where the chamber of commerce (in most of the cases) was chosen to serve as a TMO and implements the projects specified in the Basic Plan. The TMO involves residents, retail store owners, the public sector, and others with the goal to encourage revitalization activities within the DID. The TMO was designed to plan and to coordinate government urban development initiative, or to support the government initiatives. The central government is more involved in the management of the district as it decides whether or not to implement projects, whereas the TMOs are more responsible for the services they provide in the area.

Main Street Associations, or Main Street Programs are designed to address the economic decline and other threats to small and historic downtown in the United States. MSAs intend to preserve the existing economic environment as a development plan to enhance the sense of community through the improvement of public space. The leading initiator of MSA, in contrast to the BIDs, is a structure of the federal government in the United States, the National Trust for Historic Preservation, and the private sector is included as a part of the association in the classic form of BIDs, and currently (at least in Texas), provides more than half of the investments in the area. In terms of services, MSAs focus more on the design, enhancement of physical assets, and visual qualities of the district, without undermining other services as well.

4 Case Studies

4.1 Case Study 1: CID Safeguarding Banská Štiavnica

4.1.1 Background

In 1990, there were scores of deteriorated buildings in the historic part of Banská Štiavnica. Neither the state nor investors had any interest in safeguarding architectural and monuments of the state or investors. Jobs were lost, young people left town, and housing in the historic sector of town became substandard. The city government formulated the following objectives:

- Gain international recognition of the historic significance of Banská Štiavnica by registering it on UNESCO's World Heritage List.
- Ensure investors for renewal of deteriorated historic monuments and sites.
- Reclassify the town to a higher administrative level.
- Complete needed technical infrastructure.
- Create new jobs.
- Improve social infrastructure by providing conditions for permanent housing in the historic core.

The government, state bodies, universities, residents, and civic initiatives set the priorities for safeguarding the town's renewal and guaranteed the project. The city government elaborated the priorities named above in a separate document, where specific operational objectives were formulated, and resources were defined for their implementation.

In this way the concepts were prepared for safeguarding historic monuments and sites; housing in the historic core of the town; creation of new jobs; development of a water supply system. Others were building pressure zones; introducing natural gas, an electricity supply system; protecting the environment and improving the standard of living. Municipal bodies discussed and approved timing and financial resources. The next step was elaboration of the concepts into yearly operational plans.

Priority was given to mobilize human resources, especially to gain the support of residents for the project implementation. Bulletins as well as meetings were used to inform residents about the proposed changes and procedures. Meetings were also used to discuss the involvement of civic associations, volunteers, and residents. Another aspect of the mobilization of people was to gain sympathizers for the project implementation, especially from the locals, former students, weekend-cottagers, hut owners, and other people who used to visit Banská Štiavnica repeatedly. The third step was to deal with influential people in society and in politics; people who promised their support for the project proposal.

The mobilization of money was based on the principle that each owner had to upkeep his or her property to good condition to enhance the town's aesthetic image. Each owner also had to be involved in social and economic activities. All the properties in the town were divided into two groups: those needed for public functions, and the others. The others were sold on condition that buyers restored them. The income from these sales was then used for renewal of municipal buildings and public spaces.

4.1.2 Results

Since the beginning of the initiative, more than 30 historic buildings have been renewed and fully integrated in social and economic life of the town. Sixty apartments have been gained in the renovated historic buildings in addition to spaces for retail businesses and administration.

After more than 30 years the town has again become the administrative district center. National institutions were re-established and, after an 80-year break, university education returned. All this attracted new town residents, especially the intelligentsia. In the historic core of Banská Štiavnica three hotels were established that contribute to tourism development. A more environmentally friendly municipal wastewater treatment plant has been installed. Eight water reservoirs that were part of the historic water management system were rebuild in the natural environment of the town and its immediate surroundings.

The changes in the physical conditions of the town persuaded the residents of the significance and efficiency of the revitalization process for it improved housing quality, shopping services, created new jobs and recreational centers. Another effect for the town was that its social prestige within the Slovak Republic increased as did civic activities aimed at further development of the revitalization process. The results achieved contributed toward gaining the confidence of investors and state bodies that encouraged even more investment in the town.

The most significant aspect in ensuring sustainability of the results achieved and further prospective improvement of living conditions in Banská Štiavnica was to merge renovated historic objects into social and economic life of the town. With the availability of improved permanent housing in the historic buildings, young families moved in. This also provided them with new jobs in the historic buildings renovated for business, especially in shops and services. In this way, the permanent social, material, and economic life was improved.

The location of national institutions in the town center has enabled continuous contact of the historic environs with new residents. This is important for continual regeneration of information and ideas, as well as dissemination of new knowledge and positive experiences of life in Banská Štiavnica. Capacities of building companies, which in the first stage were used mostly for safeguarding and renovation of historic buildings, are utilized increasingly for maintenance of renovated monuments. This means permanent jobs in the building firms, at the same time assuring a high standard of maintenance of the renovated monuments and homes.

Environmental gains were also made; this came from the replacement of outdated heating systems of central boiler rooms from brown coal to natural gas. This in turn removed acid rainfall that had previously damaged the historic buildings. General renovations of dams within the historic water management system resulted also in the renewal of the water reservoirs which, while conserving rainwater, does not lead to a variation of the water level in the surrounding area. The existence of permanent administration and supervision of the reservoirs have resulted in efficient water management.

4.1.3 Lessons Learned

- Deteriorated historic buildings cannot be removed effectively unless there is no long-term prospective utilization corresponding to their historic significance. In addition, there will be no success if the use of these buildings is not woven into the social and economic life of a town. That is the reason why revitalization is preferable to the renovation of historic buildings. When preparing a renovation plan of a historic town-building, technical and organizational possibilities should be viewed in accordance with the long-term social and economic possibilities.

- Renovation of a dilapidated historic town cannot be forced. It is not possible to develop a revitalization program of renovation without involving the community, and without persuading of the residents, concerned governmental and non-governmental institutions. The public should not be mere bystanders; they must be direct and interested participants who contribute to the management of the processes.
- A program of town renovations should be given incentives so as to attract investors. The incentives should be based on the stability of the social and economic environment, and on guarantees of the local government about the firmness of its decisions and its conviction to achieve its plans always. The guarantees should become a part of public opinion that should support the town renovation program as the most important priority.
- When preparing and implementing a plan, home and foreign experiences should be reviewed continuously in solving problems. One must learn from one's own mistakes and those of others if the repetition of errors is to be avoided.

The lessons learned in Banská Štiavnica have been successfully replicated and adapted mainly within the Slovak Republic. Mostly only partial experiences were applied, for example safeguarding monuments and sites. Historical environment for tourism and the use of historic buildings for permanent residential housing can and should be exploited.

The important lesson generated through this project is the danger of overestimating the historic significance of monuments without making a realistic assessment of what their potential contribution to contemporary social and economic life of the town could be. Such an approach enables permanent development of historic towns. More useful is a general revitalization approach that incorporates conservation of historic monuments.

4.2 Case Study 2: URBACT Local Markets Action Plan

4.2.1 Background & Objective of the Local Action Plan

Traditionally, Barcelona's markets have formed a network of shops and commerce that distribute food produce and non-food products to inhabitants in the city. Barcelona has promoted a city model that promotes local commerce, but also the relationship side of this experience.

Shopping for foodstuffs is an integral part of Barcelona lifestyle. Markets have changed their service offer as citizens' demand and consumption patterns changed. Markets have been part of a leverage process that not only provides quality, fresh, and healthy produce, but also they have become drivers of new urban spaces and the renewal of buildings, the social integration of neighborhoods, and the creation of new economic centers in city quarters that provide quality of life. This process is managed by Barcelona's Institute of Markets (IMMB), a dedicated agency that helps stallholders professionalize their services to meet demands.

Markets are part and parcel of the city model and as such anything relevant to their future needs planning and strategy, in accordance to the needs of stakeholders. Local commerce and markets are facing challenges that range from economic competition, regulatory frames, social change, amongst others, especially given the current recession.

While markets have seen tremendous advances in terms of facility modernization and new services over the last ten years, now stakeholders involved in markets in Barcelona need to set out a vision for the next ten years taking us up to 2025, establishing objectives, stakeholder involvement, and creating indicators to measure success. The result has been a planning process that started out when Barcelona joined the URBACT Markets project. This participatory process has enabled the city to create a Local Action Plan, which has also become a strategic plan for the city's markets agency and a major city policy-planning tool.

Developing the Local Action Plan (LAP) first involved a process of diagnosis using PESTEL, SWOT analysis, and second a strategic process highlighting visions, strategic objectives, actions, and indicators to measure success. Objectives were set and each had accompanying policy measures and related actions. A participatory process was significant because of the wide impact markets have on Barcelona's social and economic networks.

The process for developing the LAP was conceived as a participatory process leveraging four types of working groups, depending on their importance in the development and operation of the plan. First, there was an inner circle formed by IMMB executive members (Barcelona's Markets Agency), and second an executive circle with IMMB representatives and 6 other key stakeholders; third, there was an advisory circle divided into three working groups: representing the soul of markets policy (renewing neighborhoods through public policy in and around markets); a group representing the driving force of markets (employment, entrepreneurship, and economic development), and finally a group representing the role of sustainability through markets (environment and proximity) with IMMB present in all working groups each formed by 6–8 people; fourth, there was a plenary circle: consisting of more than 200 people. IMMB led the participation processes. 2013 saw the diagnosis phase completed, with 2014 set aside for strategic proposals, with the plenary meeting held 2 times, advisory group meetings 12 times, the executive circle met four times, and the internal circle 5 times. Adding the 12 preparatory meetings, there have been 35 sessions with 150 people involved.

4.2.2 Main Challenges of Barcelona's Urban Markets

Political changes included the electoral mandate, which was due to run until 2015, so it was important to get support for policy actions in the strategic plan. It was also important to incorporate markets-related policies in any general political policy on retail and commercial models in Barcelona.

Economics is challenging for city markets, especially given the falls in general consumption seen over the last few years due to the recession and future difficulties likely to be encountered in terms of slow economic growth. With markets representing between 8 and 10% of all commerce and consumption, changes would affect markets hard.

Social factors represented a challenge, especially decisions about where to purchase weekly shopping and competition faced from malls. Customer loyalty needs further consideration and changing lifestyles and time constraints mean less personalized shopping environments have become popular. Social factors offer challenges but also opportunities, as long as traders are prepared to innovate. Tourism is also a challenge to traditional markets given more and more tourists are coming to the city. Certain markets see more impact – especially those in the center of town – but city markets have become a key sightseeing opportunity and their needs don't always match those of the local population or services offered by traders. Markets need to embrace new trends in consumption with market-fresh restaurants becoming increasingly popular.

Technologically, the growing trend toward electronic commerce means traditional approaches to commerce need renewing. Markets face a challenge to incorporate social media, smart commerce, and a range of other modern services that add value to shopping processes. Regulations are also a challenge, especially shop opening times which have become more relaxed. Stallholders have traditionally adopted rigid hours that are not necessarily convenient for today's shopping styles. Traders also face challenges in terms of 0 km distribution of local produce and how this might impact their businesses.

Environmental factors are providing challenges especially waste management but also the use of energy-saving technology. Distribution channels impact local communities and these include issues related to parking and electric vehicle use and in general the sustainability of innovative supply chains. Organic, ecological, and 0 km trends should be considered. Other challenges that markets face include how to strengthen collaboration between markets and surrounding high streets and retail, and the limited management skills often found amongst market traders and non-professionalized associations of traders.

5 A Study of the Tourism Improvement District in Albania

Within the last ten years, there has been a shift in the paradigm, approaches, and practices of protecting cultural heritage sites in most European countries in order to make the most sustainable and long-term use of these sites. This shift requires that these objects not only be seen as a cultural value for conservation but also as a common public asset, which, if properly rehabilitated, used and managed, can generate additional cultural, social, human, and economic capital. Moreover, such a shift created a more participatory approach, with the active involvement of communities and stakeholders, which would encourage and create a friendlier environment for tourism, visitors, and investments around heritage sites. Although these tendencies prevail in other European countries, in Albania, something like this still requires time to come because the country is characterized by almost complete state support, almost entirely public funding, and a high level of institutionalization of management of these sites and facilities.

Such a situation further complicates the involvement of other actors, such as the education sector, policy makers, business, and nongovernmental sectors in the capacity building and active involvement in the protection and management of these areas and facilities. If the preparatory actions, plans, and strategies for rehabilitation of sites and cultural heritage sites are more inclusive and offer more opportunities for participation, then they will be able to attract a broader base of knowledge, expertise, and skills from various parties and would create a sustainable and successful environment for the long-term management and use of the common heritage of the region.

The basis for such a methodology is embodied in the transformation of Korça's Old Bazaar into a pedestrian area welcoming an environment combining traditional culture with the city market, managed as a unique destination in the tourism industry, and divided into smaller environments. The overall goal is to improve management and increase the value of cultural heritage in order to exploit economic potential and promote tourism sustainable in the Old Bazaar area, in Korça, Albania.

5.1 Heritage Sites Rehabilitation

The concept of rehabilitation of cultural heritage sites is of great importance for the revitalization of the Old Bazaar in Korça because it required a combination of conservative and developmental perspectives. The first is based on the view that historical sites should be protected at the highest standard, while the second advocates the promotion of heritage sites in such a way as to maximize their contribution to the local economy but, at the same time, without sacrificing their cultural significance. Rehabilitation requires the careful adaptation of a building, a building or a historical site, for contemplative use, while also paying attention to the protection of its historical cultural values. It is a broader concept than protection or restoration because it involves regenerating the entire surrounding environment, revitalizing local communities, and capacity to contribute to economic development, stimulate tourism, create new jobs, and improve quality of life.

For this reason, the concept of rehabilitation helps all major public sector actors, such as ministries of planning, tourism and economic development, municipalities, and other funding agencies to understand that the benefit of the regeneration of cultural heritage objects can only be produced if the importance and sensitivity of individual sites and objects are taken into account and sometimes if the development models fit in as the premise for a more sustainable and secure future for as well as local communities. In the course of this paper, we will bring examples of positive practices presented thanks to the contribution of the Social Transformation Management Program (Programit të Menaxhimit të Transformimeve Sociale – MOST), the United Nations Educational, Scientific and Cultural Organization (UNESCO), and the research conducted by Europe Nostra and published in the Cultural Heritage Potentials for Europe.

5.1.1 Key Considerations from a European Perspective

Cultural Heritage Counts for Europe is an EU-funded project launched in 2013 and concluded in 2015 with an ambitious goal: collecting and analyzing existing accessible and evidence-based studies, as well as case studies on the economic, social, cultural, and environmental impacts of cultural heritage, in order to identify the value of cultural heritage recognized by the European Commission by 2014 as a strategic source for a more sustainable Europe. The final report produced by this project (Giraud-Labalte et al., 2015) presents the main conclusions and recommendations and we identified some of which could be taken into consideration for the case of the Old Bazaar in Korça:

1   Cultural heritage is a primary component and a key contributor to the attractiveness of Europe's regions, cities, towns, and rural areas, attracting foreign private investment and the development of creative cultural areas, thus contributing to an increased regional competitiveness in Europe, as well as the global competitiveness of the whole region. Studies on Dublin and the city's strategy for its "talent center" based on the resilience of the city's historic center showed that city differentiation based on its cultural heritage assets and the preservation of their authenticity contributed to attracting a class of potential young and creative workers.

2   Europe's cultural heritage provides its regions with a unique identity and compelling narrative that creates the basis for effective marketing strategies aimed at the development of cultural tourism and attracting investment. The atmosphere of a historic city, or even a single historical building, transmits the message of long-term credibility, security, support and, in many cases, prestige. Although the primary goal of the UNESCO Cultural Heritage List is to promote the protection and management of the most prestigious cultural heritage values, the inclusion in this list is widely seen as a brand and functions as a powerful promotional marketing tool. Some research conducted in Hamburg (Germany) shows that environments that are part of cultural heritage and used for business and commercial reasons, for example, a firm's offices in a historic building are generally seen as prestigious business environments. These studies showed that 87% of employees thought the atmosphere at work improved after relocating to a historic building and 73% of customers also reacted positively to such a change. Cultural heritage is an important factor in selecting a country for new investment, especially for IT businesses and those employing highly qualified staff.

3   Cultural heritage produces numerous jobs across Europe, including a wide range of occupations and skill levels that vary from work in the construction sector related to the protection, reconstruction, repair, maintenance, and restoration of these facilities to cultural tourism, small- and medium-sized enterprises (SMEs), mainly part of industries that require high creativity. The cultural

heritage sector is estimated to produce over 26.7 indirect jobs for each direct job position, a figure many times higher than, for example, the automotive industry that generates just 6.3.

4   Cultural heritage is an important source of creativity and innovation through the generation of new ideas and solutions to problems, as well as the creation of new and innovative services – from digitalization of cultural assets to the use of the most sophisticated virtual reality technologies – with the goal of expanding access of citizens and visitors to historic sites and buildings. As evidenced by the results of the EPOCH project, cultural heritage stimulates information and communication technology innovation related to the digitalization of heritage resources as well as the need to introduce them to a wider public through virtual technologies. Creating new products and services requires more specialized and quality jobs – both on the supply side and on demand.

5   Cultural heritage has proven to provide a high return on investment and is a significant generator of tax revenues for public authorities. It accomplishes this either through economic activities in sectors directly related to inheritance, as well as indirectly through investments stimulated by heritage projects. The Borgund (Norway) stave church generates, based solely on tax revenue data, 628.5% of annual return on investment.

6   Cultural heritage serves as a catalyst for sustainable heritage-based regeneration. For example, cultural heritage has played a key role in regenerating the so-called Cathedral Quarter in Belfast (Northern Ireland, United Kingdom). Investments in the areas not related to its cultural heritage produced little or no result in terms of increasing investor interest, whereas investment in heritage resulted to be an important regenerative factor for it.

7   Cultural heritage can be part of solving the challenges of climate change that is threatening Europe, for example, by protecting and regenerating the potential stored within sites and historic buildings. Maintenance and reuse of existing structures contribute to curbing excessive urban expansion, prolonging the lifespan of using buildings or parts of these buildings, and ensuring avoidance of accumulation of waste.

8   Cultural heritage contributes to the quality of life, endowed with "character" and neighborhood atmosphere, cities, and regions around Europe, transforming them into popular places to visit, live, and work – attractive for both residents and tourists or representatives of creative elites. Research conducted by the Urban Development Institute in Krakow (Poland) argues that the successful restoration of the historic centers of Polish cities has influenced

the quality of life of local populations, has given rise to tourism due to their increased attractiveness, and has improved the overall image of these cities.

9   Cultural heritage is an essential stimulus for lifelong learning and education, offering a deeper understanding of history and providing people with a sense of civic pride and sensation of belonging. It also does this by promoting personal cooperation and development. Inheritance has encouraged people who have stopped their education and qualification, for various reasons, to return to education programs and to deepen their mastery of new skills and knowledge. The Jamtli Museum in Östersund (Sweden) – the regional museum of the historic districts of Jämtland and Härjedalen in the city of Östersund – consists of an open environment surrounded by a historic building as well as a closed museum. In cooperation with the archive and the local high school, this museum initiated a program aimed at creating a positive learning experience for young people. Such an initiative succeeded and resulted in a return to school for one-third of the participants.

10   Cultural heritage combines many of the positive impacts summarized above providing social cohesion and human capital improvement for communities across Europe. It constitutes a stimulating framework for participation, integration, and incitement to integration. The relationship between a historical environment and social capital is developed through a sense of belonging to that country, driven by the presence of historic buildings. This builds the context in which interactions between people are born and strengthened. Thus, cultural heritage can be an important factor for building social capital by acting as a knot that enables the creation of "bridges" within the community, between different age groups, ethnicities, and practitioners of different faiths – either on heritage site or museums, as well as local shops, shops, or boutiques that are part of or near these areas. The volunteering programs offered by heritage protection organizations can reward their participants with benefits such as inter-generational contacts, interactions direct, and a sense of belonging. In this way, they positively influence the development of common understanding among people.

5.1.2 *Historic Markets*

Currently, the historic markets of cities face major challenges that have threatened their historical heritage and have been associated with economic stagnation as a result of rapid changes in social, economic, and ecological conditions. These markets face substantial changes in their traditional role, especially as a result of the decline of agriculture and the value of handicrafts. Likewise, the devaluation of handworks and the expansion of large food-producing networks have a profound negative impact on local communities. The lack of a balance between the development and protection of the traditional urban structure is often associated with economic stagnation or loss of the unique cultural heritage of an area. Together with it, the cultural identity fades. The examples presented in this analysis were selected to include as many market management segments ranging from defining their mission and values to the disclosure of policies, strategies, action plans and models, and managerial procedures for it. The main incentive for establishing historic markets are:

1   Local ambitions and community empowerment
2   Investments attraction and continuous development
3   The main site of the city
4   Cultural ecosystem

On the one hand stands the conservation, while on the other hand the exploitation and use of the market. This dichotomy should be based on building a symbiotic relationship between these two components. Markets were seen in the past as a source of responsibility for local authorities but today they have become a gathering place for local residents, for empowering communities and local enterprises. Whatever the direction of the strategy or the driver of the rapid spread of entrepreneurship, the most important elements of the management of these markets are vision, approach, and leadership. The benefits that such cultural markets and ecosystems bring to European cities are well-documented. Regardless of the model, market type, shape, or size, what is most important is that it meets the aspirations of the locals and their daily needs. A greater focus on the local community at the same time increases the attractive tourism market value by highlighting local values, features, and characteristics. Good and visionary management can produce multidimensional benefits to the market:

1   Economic benefits:

    a   Economic platform for the SMEs
    b   Employment opportunities
    c   Added value and profits for the locals

2   Education benefits:

    a   Engages young professional with local suppliers and places
    b   Brings together youth with the masters and craftsmen
    c   Displays actual opportunities for students to create study cases, learning projects, or places of activities

3   Health benefits:

    a   Access to more fresh and organic food
    b   Stimulates the perception of wellbeing

4   Environmental benefits:

    a   Less carbon emissions
    b   Local food network
    c   Less intense shopping but more frequent

5   Social benefits:

    a   Social environment
    b   Social inclusion of local communities
    c   Social awareness

5.1.3 *Advantages of Local Markets: A Manifesto*

In 2014, representatives of the cities of Barcelona, Venice, and Florence, as leaders in URBACT MARKETS, CENTRAL MARKETS, and MARAKANDA projects, respectively, together with the support of a number of other cities, declared the support of their municipal governments regarding the promotion of markets where both food and non-food products are sold. They initially considered their essential role in the development of local trade and, second, their catalyst role in urban regeneration and social cohesion. In sign of their commitment, the signatory cities and other parties committed themselves to actively engage in the organization of the International Market Day, expressing their support for the common vision and concept of the markets, in the manner in which will be discussed below. Moreover, in order to achieve long-term strategies, the signatory parties expressed the will to revitalize the European Network of Markets, called EMPORION, and established in Barcelona in January 2006. EMPORION was born to support and strengthen the positions of the markets in the society European dimension, as well as the important role they play in the European "builder" process. According to their "Manifesto" major and sustainable social, economic, cultural, environmental, &

health advantages exercising from the existing sector of economic and local communities include:

1 *Promotion of social inclusion.* Markets constitute an exchange point between different layers of society, generate some sense of local affiliation, play a key role in socio-cultural support, and emphasize civil values. They do this by identifying, distributing, and promoting these values.

2 *Supporting the inclusive of "community benefits".* Since they are unifying units within cities or neighborhoods they serve as a service center and integrating element for the elderly, immigrants, & people at risk of social marginalization.

3 *Employment stimulation through SMEs and enterprises.* Markets are the main actors in generating economic activity in cities, serving as structural elements of trade exchanges, responsible for generating the dynamism that characterizes business and employment. These include retailers, local producers, along with logistics and distribution companies.

4 *Economic and urban registration.* Markets are a valuable tool for more integrated and cohesive urban planning. They can be used as part of the regeneration of historic centers and rehabilitation of old neighborhoods at social, cultural, and economic levels.

5 *Promotion of culture and delivery of tourism.* Markets are the essence of the cultural heritage of any community. Thus, they act as an important attraction for local and foreign tourism by promoting the local gastronomic and culinary tradition.

6 *Environmental impact reduction.* By promoting the trade in the locality, markets enable the avoidance of using private means of transport. That way they reduce pollution and contribute to building a more integrated development city.

7 *Support security to local agriculture.* These build bridges between urban and rural, bringing the agricultural producers and craftsmen together.

8 *Inclusive production and local consumption.* Something that guarantees quality and variety of products, consumption of seasonal products, excellence, and variety in local production.

9 *Improving health citizens.* Markets play a vital role in enabling European consumers access to fresh products with affordable cost, diversity, and multiple choices. These markets also play an important role in promoting healthy eating habits, also acting as platforms for distributing relevant information to the public.

5.1.4 Local Market Policies

As an addressing example for policy development in local markets, we have selected the city of London because it has the largest number of highly rated markets. The London Market Policy Project aims to answer questions, such as: What Makes a Successful Market? Why are some markets successful while others fail? What is the role of these markets in the 21st century? The following section attempts to answer these questions, defines the relationship between policy and practice, and contains guidelines for this sector. One of the problems faced by this industry (and one of its weaknesses) is the systematic lack of information and research about these activities. For this reason, the National Association of British Markets Authorities (NAMBA), a co-operative partner in a project of the Economic and Social Research Council, based on the Research Institute for Communities and Rural Areas of the University of Gloucestershire, undertook a search titled "The traditional retail food market: the secret sector? A geographic analysis". Meanwhile, the Retail Market Alliance (RMA) set up a working group in September 2008. With the funding support of the British Council of Shopping Center Education Groups, it tried to answer some questions, such as: What is their geographical distribution? Who manages them? How often do they operate? How many traders are operating? What is the turnover of these markets? How many people are directly employed in this industry? How are the markets performing and facing the current economic recession?

Strategic priorities of Retail Market Alliance include:

1   *Promotion of policy objectives.* RMA will continue to promote the benefits of markets and, in particular, of the five policy issues where these markets make the largest contribution. It will engage with the local and central governments, the private sector, and the media, while constituent associations will provide support to each market individually.

2   *Reasons in favor of financial investments.* How can markets benefit from financial support and attract the necessary amount of investment? There are two issues to consider – the first is the identification of available funding sources, and the second with their "withdrawal" toward the markets. Funding for the development of these markets can come from different sources, whether these are individual, institutions, or combined. The main sources are local authority programs, borrowings, regeneration funds, reinvestment of market profit, partnerships with the private sector,

other commercial partnerships, available grants. However, the successful application of investment funds remains a challenge for these markets. *Business-related issues must be prepared and supported by certain data.* This issue should include policy reasons for investment, claim disclosure, costs, financial model/options, operational model/options, evidence for long-term sustainability support, risk.

3   *Managerial models.* The model of local authorities, the private sector, the model of traders, partnerships, limited liability partnerships, social enterprise, and joint management.

4   *Attracting new businesses.* Inclusion of young entrepreneurs in the sector, young people, engagement with national, regional, and local governments in order to identify support sources for business development within the market sector.

5   *Creating and strengthening relationships with key partners.* The benefits of collaboration, partnerships with the private and public-sector individuals, and organizations that can help achieve strategic priorities.

6   *Marketing and Public Relations.* Promotion of the sector at the national and regional levels.

7   *Improving managerial support.* Quality decision making, effective communication, sharpness and business wisdom, and the ability to build a safe, clean, and inviting environment are essential criteria to be met.

8   *Fulfillment of knowledge gaps at national and regional level.* National coordination, analysis and dissemination of existing data at the local market, assistance to markets that currently do not perform periodic and regular performance measurements to perform such activities.

Market management is changing and will continue to change, while new models are beginning to emerge. In particular, the small market option, managed by municipal or communal councils, where these small local authorities provide resources and management tools, provides sustainable solutions. Likewise, even the largest local authorities have begun to consider establishing joint ventures, combining public and private sectors, at regional or city level. These ensure the development of economies of scale and a clear vision for strategic planning. Partnerships with the private sector and administered markets as social ventures will also continue to develop. The challenges faced by the UK market industry are enormous. Particularly, it can be mentioned: the need to attract investment in these markets, improve management quality and supply of retailers, and attract new businesses. RMA's strategic priorities aim to address these issues and make it necessary for resources to focus on solving them.

5.2 Korça's Old Bazaar: Present & Past Uses of the Site

The Old Bazaar area (including Mirahor's mosque) is considered as the urban nucleus of the city of Korça. Although dating back to the late 15th and beginning of the 16th century, their real physiognomy was shaped during the 19th century (Kallamata, 1988), a period that corresponds with the rapid growth of the city. The Old Bazaar has played a very important role in the history of the market throughout Albania's history. Its size and liveliness are comparable only to that of Shkodra, from which no trace currently remains (Riza, 1978).

It is also known for its rapid growth (measured in terms of geographical size expansion, variety of handicraft products, and commercial activities), as well as the fact that it is the oldest Bazaar reconstructed through a specific plan and use of materials and modern techniques (Riza, 1978). For this reason, compared to the shopping of other towns, such as Kruja, Elbasan, Shkodra, etc., it is distinguished for more solid, curative, and more hygienic structures. Like other Bazaars, that of Korça, included in the past open markets, group of craftsmen, retail stores, and guesthouses or *"hane"*.

5.2.1 Site Significance

The Old Bazaar of Korça is a bearer of special urban & architectural, cultural, economic, and social values for the city and the region. As a variant of the typology of the traditional Bazaars in Albania, it is distinguished for its size, vivacity, and innovatory urban and architectonic solutions. It is special also for the variety of styles that combine local knowledge and technique with foreign influences in terms of building constructions and decorations.

At the origin of the emergence of Korça as an important urban center and situated in one of its key areas, the Bazaar has been integrated for centuries in the life of the people of Korça and has become a spiritual and cultural symbol of the city and the region.

5.2.2 Site Condition & Conservation

The ensemble of the Bazaar is in good physical condition. The last interventions (2015) have prevented eventual collapse of the existing structures. However, the original interiors of the shops as well as important details of the front shops have been lost, thus altering the visual identity and affecting the authenticity of the facades. The Bazaar is still used under its capacities, with a reported 17 shops out of 153, being currently in use (11%). The different blocks of shops are still complete for the most part, with the exception of a few of them, whose regular architectural planning shapes have been modified because of the loss of constituent buildings.

5.3 Strategic Approach

5.3.1 Preamble

Successful results of the strategic approach to markets development were shown in MARAKANDA Project implemented by nine partners including Municipality of Genoa (Italy, Liguria), Local Authorities Union of Xanthi District (Greece, Eastern Macedonia and Thrace), Municipality of Limassol (Cyprus), University of Genoa – Research Centre in Town Planning and Ecological Engineering (Italy, Liguria), Municipal Institute of Markets of Barcelona (Spain, Cataluña), PLURAL – European Study Centre (Italy, Liguria), Municipality of Favara (Italy, Sicilia), National Research Centre (Egypt), Souk El Tayeb (Lebanon).

The overall objective of the Marakanda Project was to foster the social and economic development of the partner cities by creating a cluster of historic city markets through strengthening relationships among them, improving governance and synergies among public institutions, market operators and experts, and valorizing high-quality agro-food and artistic handicraft productions.

These terms were a fundamental reference for the drawing up of the list of recommendations: they were organized following the approach purposed by the Institute of the Markets of Barcelona about the selection of the best practices, that in order to support continuity of analysis and methodology and for facilitating the work by partners. They chose to list the collected practices according to a prioritization of five categories of interest: infrastructures and urban planning, services, management, promotion & communication, farmers' markets and enhancing of local products.

Within this project, a framework was formulated in which three strategies "save", "act", and "look" were referred to three periods of time and that, together, try to respond to the general interrogative of the guidelines: *"What could be useful to do today?"*

"SAVE" represents all is necessary to do for preserving your past and tradition (recent or very ancient). Recognizing the value an experience had is the first step: afterward, you can decide to implement the answer to the current and future needs building up on a previous situation that is not (only) a constraint but a potentiality or even a resource inherited from the past for your development. "ACT" is the action for excellence: you have to intervene without being in late, keeping decisions, and without leaving opportunities. Here, are gathered all the suggestions that can be useful having in mind to improve our present. Some options might be at your disposal in order to score the same goal, but probably one is more adequate for your condition and better respond to the question.

"LOOK" is an innovative category, in a certain way, because it purposes, from now onwards, a systematic and critical review of what you are ordinarily making for your markets' improvement. The guidelines in this column would like to address your activity in monitoring evolutions and individuate which are the main aspects/features/actors/processes/opportunities to be attentive to from now and along the coming years.

5.3.2 Guidelines

5.3.2.1 Services

ACT:

- Put attention to your waste!
- Choose your timetable!
- What about a post office?!
- Be a provider of local jobs!
- One market leads to another!

LOOK:

- Not only take-away: consider the cooking option!
- Remember that waste is a crucial aspect of your future!
- Become a gatherer of the community!
- Think about renewable energy for your markets!
- Increase market's competitiveness vs. hyper and supermarkets!
- What about evening openness?
- The future in the home delivery!

5.3.2.2 Urban Planning and Infrastructure

SAVE:

- The architectonic features of the market are interesting not only for the sector value but also for the attractiveness it has for non-expert people.
- Don't forget how people traditionally reach you!
- Integrate new consumers' behaviors with old-functioning systems!

ACT:

- Consider urban accessibility!
- Strategic planning for your market!
- Make your market a catalyst of change!
- Take the opportunity of remodeling for upgrading your status!
- Make your market "different"!
- Take care of the connection between indoor and outdoor stalls!

LOOK:

- List indicators on markets in the monitoring of your strategy!
- Measure the direct and indirect impacts of a market on its neighborhood!
- Plan a market!
- Intercept best practices in planning activities!
- Be attentive with the times of the regeneration project!
- Take care of your profits to be re-invested!

5.3.2.3 Management

SAVE:

- Preserve your feasts!
- Integrate with your retailing community!

ACT:

- Catch up with the projects' financing!
- Consider the opportunity of a financial sharing!
- Choose your public/private partnership model!

- Working group: join a table!
- Act in the "green" community!
- Take the occasion of a seasonal/feast recurrence!
- Be present in your "healthy community"!

LOOK

- Integrate markets into town center management!
- Make your markets a safe keeper!
- Measure your performances!
- Provide a development business model!
- Invest in projects' fundraising!
- Working group: make the table "stable"!
- Be prudential with loans!
- Invest in research!

5.3.2.4 *Promotion and Communication*

SAVE:

- Link with your traditional food festivals!

ACT:

- Be present in the "green" community!
- Measure your customers' footfall!
- School at the market!
- Share best practices!
- Make your market "different"!
- Make your market a cultural offer!
- Take care of the internal communication!
- Develop shared successful strategies for marketing and communication!

LOOK:

- Take care of the internal communication!
- Do not forget creative people!
- Evaluate TV and radio advertisement!
- Boost and communicate the social impact of the markets!
- Invest in smart communication!

5.3.2.5 Farmers Markets & Enhancing of Local Products

SAVE: Face current supply challenges with old farmer's markets!
ACT:

- Not only a farmer market!
- Develop "green" and local brands!

LOOK: Enhance the rural-urban cooperation!

5.3.3 Management Models

The following presentation on a variety of management models and approaches is taken from the analysis conducted within the Med Emporion project. This project is promoted and led by the cities of Torino, Barcelona, and Genova, together with de Conservatoria dell Piemonte and the Conservatoire des Cuisines de la Mediterranée of Marseille. The general goal of the project is to study the importance of food markets in the Mediterranean area as a tool of urban development and economic promotion and to undertake research about the importance of the product of proximity and the role of the market as a tool for social cohesion.

In this project, three types of municipal market network management models were identified: public, private, and mixed. Public management corresponds to direct management of the facilities by the municipal public authority; mixed management involves the joint participation of a private company or a traders' association through an agreement with the local public authority; and the public model is where markets are directly managed through private initiative.

Barcelona. The markets of Barcelona are managed by a Council body, the Institut de Mercats Municipals de Barcelona (IMMB), which through the market manager controls, among others, administrative, functional, and commercial aspects. Despite being a public model, it has aspects that bring it close to the mixed model.

Beirut. The two markets in Beirut have special characteristics in their management, which is private in both cases. There is no type of management or control by the public authorities of the products sold. Managers constantly promote local products and direct sales between producers and consumers.

Cairo. Rather than shaping a new system of management and promotion of markets (health regulations, commercial promotion, or market management), the body aims to recover the historical heritage.

In the near future, another objective will be the control of prices and quality.

Castellón. The global management of municipal markets has been the responsibility of the Traders' Association, while the City Council is responsible for the maintenance of buildings.

FES. The existence of craft guilds suggests the existence of traders' associations structured by type of selling.

Genoa. The management of the markets in Genoa is public. The Council is responsible for granting the licenses to traders (it rents the public space and the facilities) and the infrastructures.

Istanbul. In the case of Istanbul there are two models:

- Street markets (Bazaar), whose management is considered to be shared by the district councils and the chambers of commerce.
- The Spice Market is jointly managed by a traders' association which, through a manager, manages the security and the common maintenance of the services.

Ljubljana. A public company is responsible for the management, maintenance, and cleaning of all the markets included in the municipal network. Moreover, it is responsible for renting the facilities located outside the Central Market and the storage of the merchandise used in the respective commercial activities.

Turin. The markets of Turin differ according to the management mode:

- Public: managed by the Council through a body of its own, the Settore Mercati della Città di Torino.
- Mixed: managed by cooperatives.

Valencia. According to the regulations in force, the management of the markets is carried out through two modes:

- By the municipal authority, through the responsible Department at Valencia City Council.
- In a mixed mode, which is the most common, management is assumed by the Traders' Association. This model is regulated through a self-management agreement between the association and the Council.

Zagreb. In Zagreb the model is public; the management of the network of the 23 markets is carried out by a department of the Council called Zagrebacki holding.

5.4 Issues

5.4.1 Site Presentation & Interpretation

There is no information table in the main entrances of the area with relevant information about its history, meanings, or other information that would facilitate the engagement of the visitors, citizens, and users. The shops, bearers of meaningful histories, and data with local, national, and regional relevance, lack information about it. The commercial signage seems to have been standardized and based on motifs, patterns, and concepts that are not grounded in the local context or the specificities of each commercial activity (type of shops). *The historic names of the streets have been replaced.* The Bazaar is presented and promoted in various Korça city guides produced and disseminated in the last years such as "Your key to Korca" (2010) or "The photographic guide of the region of Korça" (2011).

5.4.2 Education

General information about the cultural heritage monuments in Korça is presented in the framework of the national curricula for lower and higher education. Presentation of specific information or themes in relation to the old Bazaar in Korça or that of other cities is absent. General information – mostly a historic perspective of the Bazaar – could only be found in "My birthplace: Korça and Devolli". Thëllimi and Larti (2008), a specific publication that is part of the national curricula and that is used for the 5th Grade of the nine-year schools.

5.4.2.1 Factors Impacting on Heritage & Risk Assessment

The *natural risks* are considerable, especially in the case of the rough climate of Korça, characterized by important quantities of snow and rain, which can provoke serious damages to structural elements of the buildings. Considering this type of risk, the decision to leave some of the facades in the Bazaar uncovered (not plastered) is questionable (it also seems problematic in regard to the historical accuracy and thus the authenticity of the monuments).

Fire risks should also be mitigated – fire having already destroyed the Bazaar at least three times in the past. The usage of more sustainable construction materials and techniques during the last reconstruction (the last major fire was in 1879) would not suffice to prevent entirely this type of risk. The installation of hydrants is one of the legal requirements to comply with (requirements are listed in the law no 8766, date 5.4.2001 for Fire Prevention and Safety).

Traffic and parking management seems to be a concern for the shop-keepers and users of the area. Balancing the needs related to the successful operation of the businesses (shops supply, limited traffic hours, etc.) and the prerequisites related to the long-term preservation of the site should be granted priority. There is a lack of parking space near the Bazaar, and this might affect the frequentation of the Bazaar. A parking system located in the periphery of the Bazaar could be beneficial. The axis at the entrance of the Bazaar "Fan Noli Boulevard", one of the main roads in the city is a constant source of fluxes that can harm the existing structures (indirect impact, irreversible) and polluting gases that contribute to creating acid rains that can also irremediably affect the historic buildings (indirect impact, cumulative and long-term effect). Softer motilities should be encouraged (biking, carpooling) and more efficient organization of the bus line(s) that serve the Bazaar would be also helpful.

Man factor has been for a long time one of the biggest threats mainly because of the abandonment of the area and its illegal use. However, nowadays this type of risk is not entirely mitigated, and the challenges related to it are and will be coming from the decision-making, namely the ability to find *an adequate balance between revitalization and conservation of the area.*

In these terms, important questions need to be addressed, namely:

- *Planning of the remaining infrastructural works* related to the connection of public utilities is implemented as soon as a business is implanted in one of the shops of the Bazaar. To avoid the negative externalities, intervention block per block is recommended. A better communication needs to be established a priority with responsible institutions (Municipality, DRKK), the construction companies, and the specialized operators (OSHEE-electricity supply, UKKO-water supply) to minimize the negative impact on the heritage values, attractiveness, and the current use of the area for economic purposes.
- *Physical interventions allowed/disallowed*: All proposals for intervention in the area and their foreseen effects should be carefully considered and validated a priority by the responsible institution, DRKK of Korça, according to the criteria defined by the national and local legislation.
- The preparation of *building design guidelines* pertaining to both interventions on the exterior and the interior of the shops would

precede the needed interventions and thus help the preservation of the values of the Bazaar while increasing awareness of the shop-keepers/owners/users of the monuments.

- *Optimization of available space*: In many cases the underground storages (and supporting aeration windows) have been permanently closed after the 2015 renovation, thus resulting in a loss of functional space. The historic "storage" function is still nowadays a major need, be it for businesses or for other activities to be held in the Bazaar. In many cases, shopkeepers/owners have tried to make the underground storages functional again, resulting often in aggressive interventions on the buildings or their surroundings.
- *Threats to visual identity and functional harmony*: In the perspective of an increased rate of shops active in the Bazaar, the commercial/urban furniture and supporting equipment should be regulated a priority (via a collocation plan) in order to avoid unnecessary obstruction or damaging to the facades, the public space, and the regular exercise of the daily business activities. The regulation should include not only the main square of the Bazaar but should also apply to the entire area.
- *Alterations to the historic front shops*: Natural factors and human activities resulted in an aggravated loss of the historic element of the front shop such as rollers (qepena, or rolo), decorative elements of the fascia and pilasters, railings, etc., that have resulted in the change of the overall atmosphere (see below). Besides, up to now, we haven't been able to find consistent graphic/visual documentation of the historic features of the workshop, which means that their eventual loss would be irreversible. The visual standards of the front shops in the Bazaar should be treated carefully by combining the need to create an attractive landscape and atmosphere, with the need to preserve the authenticity of the shops and the Bazaar area as a whole. Commercial signage should be the object of regulation a priority, in order to avoid the proliferation of materials, concepts, and positioning in regard to the facades. Specific guidelines on the design and maintenance of the historic front-shops should be issued as a way to both regulate their use and enhance understanding of their values.
- *Lack of maintenance*: Even though the renovation works have recently finished, the first signs of the lack of regular maintenance and cleaning are appearing. A maintenance program and plan should be prepared and disseminated among the different actors. A multiactor engagement is needed for financing maintenance as well as conservation efforts. Reliance only on the shops (or on the

public sector only) is unsustainable. The chosen financial mechanisms should be carefully designed and explained so that they are not perceived from current/future businesses as an unnecessary burden to their activities.

- *Weak local awareness about the values of the bazaar*: Repeated vandalism acts (for example steal of new gutters or other elements of the front-shops) or the dysfunctional waste management (besides businesses, several families still live in the area) requires a well-thought awareness-raising campaign as a necessary complement to the physical works and changes in the regulations.
- *The negative image of the bazaar*: The recent history of the area but also the latest interventions, and related lack of information keep the local inhabitants from integrating the Bazaar area into their daily or recreation/leisure practices. Furthermore, businesses in the area are operating only until 14:00, after which the Bazaar becomes a very quiet and unpopulated area. This also prevents the local inhabitants from frequenting it after their school/work time. A marketing strategy should be devised, including a branding component and the complementary "profile-raising" events.
- *The ownership issue*: Use and/or maintenance of the buildings in the Bazaar has to deal with multiple and often absentee owners. Experience indicates that in this specific context, historical property owners would tend to consider in priority windfall profit (renting out, selling the properties) above the renewal of their value.
- *The risk of an artificial historic bazaar and gentrification*: The local regulation that limits the type of businesses that can operate in the Bazaar may have negative implications on many levels and thus affect the functioning of the ensemble on the medium and long terms. The priority accorded to service-oriented businesses above production/craft activities may affect the attractiveness of the area, especially for those tourists (foreign and locals) driven by the wish to acquire tourism products and experiences based on local traditional techniques or processes of production and commercialization (which are in the same time the main reason to visit a historic market). It also puts the businesses in the Bazaar in direct competition among each other's and in the same market niches or pushes them to compete with established businesses, such as the "Pazari i Korçës" shopping mall located also in the heart of the Bazaar. Second, this regulation leads to an irreversible deracination of some of the historic activities in the Bazaar. Some of the businesses are operating in the area from generations, their continued presence in a revitalized Bazaar is invaluable as

they contribute enormously to the "spirit of the place" and to the local tradition of entrepreneurship and craftsmanship.

The current trend of the relocation within the Bazaar of entrepreneurs and/or branches of businesses registered elsewhere is certainly a good sign. But, if not properly regulated – by striking a good balance with incentives for the local shopkeepers and craftspeople to stay or further develop their activities – it may also result in the replacement of the existing social and spiritual values with actors and activities who do not identify with the local heritage and who wouldn't necessarily allocate the means to support it.

5.5 Operational Plan

5.5.1 General Management Considerations

- The target is the revival of the reconstructed bazaar area. The old bazaar was evacuated, and the buildings have been renovated.
- 120 shops, including two hotel locations and a big stone building, are available for rent. Up to now only 20% of the locations have been rented out. At the moment, there is virtually no consumer traffic.
- The concept developed in this management plan is completely different from the proposals made by IRPP/SAAH. The IRRP/SAAH concept contains no economically sound strategy and is far too optimistic

5.5.2 Priority Target Segments

The bazaar in Korça has traditionally been a place of daily consumption for local citizens (both from Korça as well as the outlying villages). With the change in design – as well as considering its historical position and evolution – the bazaar has gained interest as a tourist attraction. As a tourist attraction, a destination such as the Bazaar will have to have two things:

1 Interesting architecture to showcase the tradition of the city or the country (thus provide sightseeing opportunities for tourists).
2 Or be a place of daily consumption, a testament of the daily life of locals (so that the daily routines are the attraction for tourists).
3 Or be both.

As part of this management plan, and after careful and thoughtful analysis, the bazaar in Korça will prosper if a combination of both options 1 and 2 above is provided for. This means that the bazaar retains some of its original functions as a place of everyday local business, as well as cater to foreign visitors due to its architectural and historical appeal. The analysis found further in this report will reveal why this choice makes sense. In addition, this conviction is quantified further to reveal that purely from a cost-benefit analysis, diverting the bazaar into a purely touristic attraction is definitely not feasible financially, but a *combination* of both touristic and utilitarian functions would be best.

The target groups to which to cater to should be the following: tourist destination, rather than a utilitarian destination. The bazaar is an attraction because it is a testament of the life of Korça. To reflect the life of Korça, the bazaar has to offer products and services for everyday use to the local citizens and to the citizens from the villages outlying the city. Thus, the list of priorities will include:

1   Local customers directly from the city of Korça
2   Local customers from outlying villages
3   Local Albanian tourists
4   Foreign tourists (Figure 5.1).

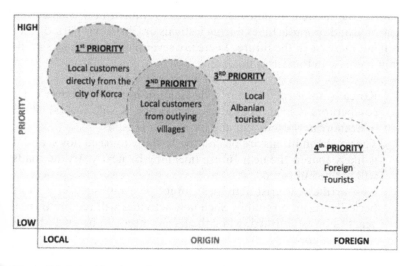

Figure 5.1 Prioritization of targeted market segments.
Source: Author illustration.

The reasoning behind setting these priorities are several:

1   The bazaar will benefit from the purchasing power of clients that are closer to the venue. Thus, proximity to the place of business is of utmost importance. This means locals directly from the city, and villagers from rural areas nearby. This is a universal fact of purchasing behavior for commodities.
2   The local population of Korça is by far the biggest group (85.000 inhabitants). They shop daily and the same customers lost their main and major source of purchase when the old market was closed.
3   The villagers are the second biggest group (50.000 people) with the same consumer behavior as the local citizens of Korça. They also lost their main and major source of purchase when the bazaar was closed.
4   Local and foreign tourists are third and fourth priority groups, respectively. By analyzing consumer behavior, we observe that both these groups do not spend much money outside their packages or hotels and accommodation deals. A closer look at their behavior reveals that they are typically in town for weekends and during the holiday season.

In the calculations that follow, we show how these two groups are insufficient to bring enough funding to the bazaar to make the bazaar tourist-centric: the number of tourists in Korça is limited (not considering seasonal and sporadic hikes during festivals or Christmas period), and will not increase in the future. There are several reasons why a significant increase in tourists is not likely:

1   Korça is an attractive tourist destination in itself, however close competitors (Ohrid, Pogradec, Gjirokastër, Krujë, coastal cities) offer more at the moment and have wider seasons.
2   The road conditions are prohibitive to daily tourism flows, and it is likely that in the near future (meaning by next year) the roads will not be improved.
3   New artificial tourist activities cannot be established in a short period and run profitably. Such new activities will require three+ years to be established, while the bazaar needs to be up and running right now.
4   The bazaar as a tourist destination in itself is by far not sufficient. The whole city will have to have a greater tourism profile so that visitors come for Korça, and visit the bazaar as a result, not the other way around.

5.5.3 What Immediate Implications Does This Bring from the Bazaar?

In order to guarantee sustainability and a steady flow of cash for local shopkeepers, relying solely on Tourism would be unrealistic. Locals' purchasing power is the most significant source of income for small entrepreneurs centered around the bazaar area, as foreign tourists form only an additional part of it. Nevertheless, laying the ground for a more sustainable model would require a higher margin of products, which is realistically feasible only if marketing plans target primarily locals.

5.5.3.1 Conclusion on Target Segmentation

As outlined above, a clear priority should be given to locals from Korça and outlying villages. This is important because it will determine the major functions and shop clustering of the bazaar. Next, Albanian tourists that visit Korça on the weekends should be 3rd priority, and then foreign tourists should be the last priority.

One important note: Korça is likely to become increasingly popular as a tourism destination in the future. However, to reach that point it will require a 10x increase in tourists per year for the next ten years. Since timing is of the essence in the bazaar, this scenario can be considered at a later stage. Thus, for now, concentrate on the clients already there.

5.5.4 Important Considerations

- The bazaar requires high traffic and a high volume of customers. Only the local/regional population can provide this.
- The bazaar requires a high percentage of high margin products. Only local fresh food and local service (market and restaurants) can provide this.
- Tourists are not a relevant group, as they are too few and they do not buy the relevant products.
- The strategy has to be focused on locals and their daily needs.

5.5.5 Strategy Adopted to Achieve this Vision

Strategy: Facelift

- Not entirely different products from the old bazaar, but the better display, better presentation, and better service.
- The products and services offered should attend to the regular local needs (Figure 5.2).

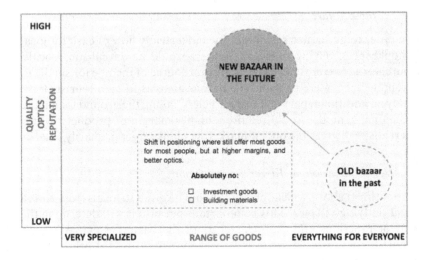

Figure 5.2 Facelift strategy and prospective positioning of the Old Bazaar of Korça.
Source: Author illustration.

The bazaar should be an upgraded substitute of the old market, not something entirely different. This means a wide range of consumer goods and services and a medium price/quality approach.

Quality means not primarily the quality of products, but the quality of the display, presentation, and service as well. A facelift is required, not a complete change of activities. The facelift of the buildings is already under way, so the facelift of the shops has to follow.

This strategy implies several important things, which some may seem very counterintuitive. A facelift strategy allows butchers, break makers, sausage, and cheese makers to still be in the bazaar and sell their products. They just need to do so in a more esthetical, hygienic, appealing, and serviceable manner.

5.5.6 Clustering

Next in this analysis are two important issues:

1   What functions should reside in the bazaar and how many for each function?
2   Where should these shops be spatially located?

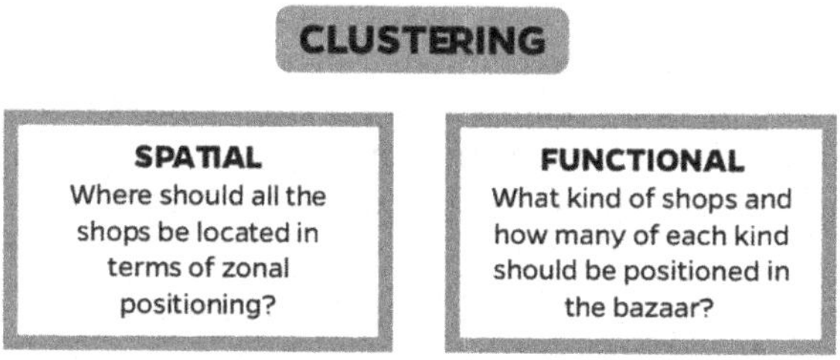

Figure 5.3 Clustering strategies.
Source: Author illustration.

This, clustering in this report is considered dual:

- **Spatial** Where should all the shops be located in terms of zonal positioning?
- **Functional** What kind of shops and how many of each kind should be positioned in the bazaar? (Figure 5.3)

5.5.6.1 Functional Clustering: Shop Mix Proposal

5.5.6.1.1 *INITIAL REMARKS*

- Numbers below are indicators, not mandatory, however, they provide a good estimation of distribution, considering similar bazaars in the world as well as the former structure of shops in the old bazaar before the intervention.
- Eat/Buy combinations are listed as restaurants and bars and include seat ins, fast foods, and all sorts of food services.
- Additionally ATMs, Toilets are services not included in the shop mix below but are add-ons that will complement the entire area.

Note on the hotels/B&B: The two hotels/B&B's have to fit into this concept. They should have a similar concept:

- 3 star, good accommodation but not over the top.
- Atmosphere is more important than function.
- Mandatory are private bathrooms, reception/common room/ breakfast room. No other meals should be served. Drinks/coffee should be always available.

The main feature of any bazaar/shopping mall/pedestrian zone is traffic. The more people, the longer they stay, the more they buy. Potential customers will avoid empty locations. So, creating traffic fast and permanently is the main demand. The proposed events (Table 5.1) are not a feature in itself, but a marketing instrument to create more traffic and to promote not only the bazaar but also the city of Korça.

5.5.6.2 Spatial Clustering: Zonal Distribution Proposal

Opposite to this demand is the second important feature: clustering. The same type of shops should be in the same micro location, to enable customers to be aware of the products and to be able to compare (agglomeration effect). Micro locations are streets with similar themes: for example, the artisan street, or the meat and fish street.

Table 5.1 Where goes what: spatial clustering of the businesses.

Restaurants/ bars	• About 15–18 have to be clustered around the central square.
	• 6–9 have to be distributed all over the bazaar, preferably at the entrances.
Service facilities	• Should be distributed erratically all over the bazaar, as a concentration of offices would be boring and not attractive
No food:	• Should be separated from the food sector and placed in the south/southwest sector of the bazaar.
	• Textile/shoe activities should be placed near the shopping mall, to add to the agglomeration effect (H3, B22)
	• Electronics should be placed at B21
	• Household appliances should be placed at H4
	• Souvenirs/local carpets/seasonal goods (sunglasses, umbrellas, gloves) should be offered close to the central square and the restaurant area.
	• B12-14 and backside B20 are potential locations for stationary.
	• B5, B18, B19 are the area for cosmetics and body care.
Food/drinks	• This sector has to be placed in the east corner and near the park for easy access by delivery vehicles.
	• This segment packed goods, fruit/vegetables, meat fish have to be separated for logistic and hygienic reasons.
	• The fish sector should be H5, B28.
	• If H5 will become a hostel (success is questionable), the fish section can be concentrated in B28 and B27.
	• Meat should be sold in B1, B2, and B16.
	• Fruit/vegetables should be offered in B3, B8, B11, B12, and B8.
	• Packaged goods should be placed in sector B17, B4, and B10.

To attend to both (partly contradicting) features, *a three-step approach* of the renting process is mandatory:

1 Define and approve the final concept of clusters (for proposal – see map and spatial clustering below)
2 Rent out shops first in one street, then the next, and so on. No dispersed rentals (one here, one there).
3 As soon as the bazaar is fully rented out, relocate the stores that do not fit into the concept; write this down in the rental agreement. For instance, if there is a butcher in the artisan street, relocate him/her in the meat and fish street once a new shop is available.

It is important to ensure flexibility within limits to cater to the shop-keeper's wishes and to fill the bazaar. We can temporarily locate a butcher in the artisan street, for instance, just to fill that street up. But later, once the bazaar is fully occupied, a reorganization may have to occur to provide for a clear shop distribution.

5.5.6.3 Map: Spatial Clustering

Source: Author illustration.

The final decision maker is the customer: the shopkeeper. The organization (city council) has no decision-making power if the supply of shops exceeds the demand (Figure 5.4; Table 5.1).

So, the locations have to be sold actively fast. This means:

1 Developing a marketing strategy to promote the location actively;
2 Make the application process as easy and fast as possible by establishing a management organization which is the only partner of the potential shopkeepers;
3 Be pragmatic, if necessary expand the interpretation of the concept, the priority is to fill up the shops fast;
4 Be patient: it will take years to fully establish the concept permanently.

5.5.7 *Marketing Activities for the Bazaar*

As the bazaar is mainly open for the local population, permanent marketing activities can be realized at a comparatively low level. Most important are activities to sell the location to potential shopkeepers.

• Create a website as a section of the Korça website that promotes the Bazaar from the customers (shopkeepers) view.

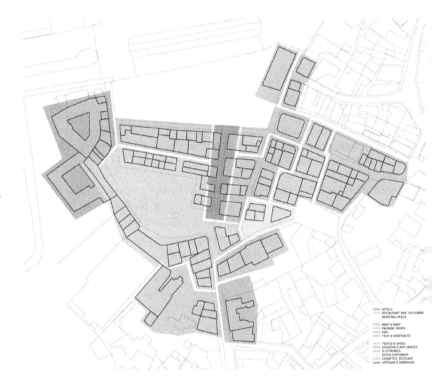

Figure 5.4 Map of the spatial clustering.
Source: Author illustration.

- Create a presentation (paper concept) for the shopkeepers. Most important here are calculation examples for the shopkeepers: How much will they pay to be there annually, and what is the potential turnover.
- Present the final concept to all retail businesses and the local consumers in a central meeting, open for everybody. Cover the meeting by local and regional media.
- Erect signs not only in the bazaar but in the city to guide people into the bazaar (as a reminder for the locals). If possible, relocate the bus station closer to the bazaar for easy access.
- Reorganize and realize a "Grand Opening", when *most of the shops are open* (music, special offers, colorful decoration).
- Organize and realize events depending on the seasons and products (Spring Market, Summer Males, Christmas Market, Wine Festival, Beer Festival, Cheese Festival) on the central square. *An inflation of festivals must be avoided.*

- Additionally, low-key music performances of local or regional artists are always possible on a daily basis.
- A regional or national festival/cultural event will take a long time to become established. Therefore, it is not a priority and may be established later.
- Produce wooden huts that should be decorated depending on the type of event.
- Develop a logo and a claim to promote the bazaar (for example: "Korça Bazaar – Relaxed Shopping and Real Fun"). Use it for all activities from stationery to flyers. It has to be part of every individual activity of the shopkeepers.
- If the rent is too high for the shopkeepers, a budget can be set to co-finance the rent for a given period of time, till the business runs smoothly (one year should be more than enough).

5.6 Bazaar Organization & Management

All activities concerning the bazaar should be concentrated in *one-newly-association*:

- This association should be the intermediate between the political institutions and the shop owners/keepers.
- Its main tasks are:
  - organizing the application process,
  - organizing the legal activities,
  - ensuring the always full occupation of the shops,
  - planning and realizing all marketing activities, and
  - helping shop owners and shopkeepers with all operative problems.
- Three professional employees should be sufficient to run the association in a company way.
- The association should have a budget, financed by the city or/and the contributing funds. In the future, it is possible, that the shopkeepers could add to the budget, too.

The organization that organizes and runs the bazaar should be a full-time professional association, not an association. Three people should run it:

1 *A CEO* who is responsible for all activities, organizes the marketing events, the legal work, and keeps contact with the shop owners and the city council,
2 *An office manager* who is responsible for all paperwork,
3 *A caretaker* who is the face toward the shopkeepers.

The organizations should be able to cover their costs but do not have to make a profit. The calculation is as follows:

1   Three people earn appx. $12.240 per year total, assuming a $340 monthly gross salary
2   Plus, a normal $5.000 marketing budget results in appx. $17.240 total costs to run the organization for one year with three people bazaar maintenance (similar to the condominium fee residents pay in their apartments).

However, payment of the fee should be a win-win approach. For their contribution, the shopkeepers get:

1   Organizing the legal activities from application to contract signing
2   Real estate management similar to the TEG management company (ACREM)
3   Marketing activities and events to promote the location
4   Personal advice and consulting to perform better

The shop owner should contribute a percentage of one month's rent to the association (as they do in real estate agencies), if they have their location rented out by the organization (this income is not included in the above calculation, as it is more a symbolic amount).

5.7 An Alternative Scenario

5.7.1 Shopping Villages

Why shopping villages? Tourist shopping villages are small towns and villages that base their tourist appeal on retailing, often in a pleasant setting marked by historical or natural amenities. They are found along touring routes, in destination areas, and near urban centers, but are markedly different from urban business and shopping districts in terms of their small scale, specialty retailing, and a distinct ambiance. Tourist shopping villages are a growing phenomenon in many destinations and can be an important tool for regional development.

Most of the shopping villages include factories/retail outlets, where out-seasoned goods can be found at discounted prices, which attracts a large number of customers. Additional factors also add to the value of a shopping village, including distinctive offers, a wide range of products, additional amenities, like parking spaces, food and leisure services, etc. In order to attract visitors, many of the shopping villages offer additional benefits to the customers. Examples include:

- Benefits for members of frequent-flyer programs of specific airline companies (e.g., Miles & More customers can earn additional miles by purchasing goods in a number of shopping villages in Europe or can spend their previously earned miles in those villages. The same stands for other frequent-flyer programs, like Asia Miles, Etihad Guest, etc.)
- Discounts and other benefits and savings are also offered to customers of local transportation companies, tour operators and travel agents, rail companies, hotels and group travel organizers, car hire companies and auto clubs, etc.
- Benefits for customers of partner banks and financial companies (e.g., American Express and several banks offer discounts to their customers in a Chic Outlet Shopping chain in Europe)
- Memberships or VIP customer status, that provide surprise gifts, tailored offers, exclusive savings, invitations to new season launches and boutique openings, access to Private Sales, and other benefits to registered members
- Tax savings for customers coming from other countries, depending on the local tax legislation (e.g., customers from non-EU countries can claim tax return on purchases at the Chic Outlet Shopping chain).

5.7.1.1 *Tourist Versus Local Residents' Expenditure*

Various researches show that tourist shopping villages are associated with destination experience, extended leisure, and self-indulgence/self-development. Most of these studies have focused only on tourist shoppers with only one study directly comparing tourist and local residents' expenditure across a range of shopping locations. This comparison found that overall at any one location tourists spend less than locals as they mix shopping with a range of other activities.

Furthermore, one group of tourists seek more intensive encounters with local culture and greater authenticity in shopping villages, such as a variety of stores and novel, unique, authentic, and distinctive products, especially these are not available at home; attractive prices/value for money; interesting windows, and product displays; easily accessible shopping areas in terms of location, having a pedestrian focus, and extended opening hours; safe and secure environments; opportunities to experience local culture; shops combined with leisure and entertainment activities; cheerful, colorful, and lively settings; streetscapes with a variety of attractive facades.

A number of studies have explored product characteristics including authenticity. While tourists purchase a wide range of goods there is a clear emphasis on buying quality and/or local, unique, and distinctive products.

5.7.1.2 The Importance of Location and Tourism Coach Package

If a village is included on a standard tourism coach package, particularly from large urban centers, then its presence as an economically sustainable year-round tourist shopping village is more assured. Two outstanding examples of the powerful presence of the coach tourism market among the studied villages are Adare in Ireland and Volendam in the Netherlands.

The notable feature of Volendam is that it's been included in day tours from Amsterdam. It lies within convenient one-hour travel time from both the center of Amsterdam and Schiphol airport and its success is in part due to the combination of easy access and its extensive presentation of diverse and traditional Dutch themes and stereotyped products. Adare is equally impressive in the arrangements which local council has constructed: large, but discrete parking area, plenty of toilet facilities, and service center for coaches. There are many other shopping villages in Ireland which feature the same attractive craft shops and gardens, but Adare's success is its provision for the coach market as well as its centrality to those visitors arriving at the Shannon airport.

5.8 Conclusions

The aim of the benchmark study is to help improve the management and sustainable development of the tourism district in the Old Bazaar in Korça (Albania). The examples recognized as successful practices by UNESCO and Europa Nostra analyzed in this research offer the stakeholders of the Korça Old Bazaar feasible options, good practices, and models to draft the future action plan for sustainable development of this historic site. It is important to underline that this benchmark study analyzes the examples from the field of the heritage sites rehabilitation, historic markets, and tourist shopping villages since no quality examples were found that were completely applicable to the Old Bazaar in Korça. Furthermore, the selection of successful practices and examples was hindered due to different expectations of diverse stakeholders of the Old Bazaar in Korça.

This study shows that the revival of the Old Bazaar in Korça is deeply intertwined with the concept of rehabilitation of cultural heritage. Conservation of the old bazaar will not only help the town of Korça to regain its cultural significance, but it will also contribute to its local economy. To underline this standpoint, this study showcases the Banská Štiavnica example since it shares many similarities with Korça. Furthermore, the ten key findings of the EU-funded project Cultural Heritage Counts for Europe (CHCfE) which was launched in 2013 to underline the importance of cultural heritage as a key contributor to the economy in Europe, and its identity was shown in this study as guidelines to planning further development of the Old Bazaar in Korça.

The study also points out the social, economic, and ecologic challenges to the historic city markets today which led to their rapid stagnancy. The decline of markets' traditional role, concerning the decline of agriculture and the value of the artisans' creations, was examined together with the imbalance of progress and preservation of the historic urban fabric since those often lead to either their economic stagnancy or the loss of the unique cultural heritage and with it the loss of identity.

Examples shown in this study were also selected to cover different segments of markets' management, starting from defining markets' mission and values to outlining their policies, strategies, management models, procedures, and action plans. As an example of policy development, this study points out to the London Markets Policy project. The Marakanda Project was shown to underline the importance of creating a cluster of historic city markets through strengthening partnerships between various cities, improving governance among public institutions, and market operators and experts.

Since clear procedures for each segment of activity are of paramount importance to ensure further development of the Old Bazaar in Korça, this study also points out one of the procedures developed by NAMBA as a helpful guideline to the stakeholders. The action plan drafted for the markets in Barcelona within the URBACT project was shown as an example of a sustainable pragmatic solution that integrated economic, social, and environmental dimensions which can also be applied to the Old Bazaar in Korça.

Successful examples of shopping villages in Europe known to combine local culture-based products and contemporary market demands were showcased to underline the importance of the strategic approach to their development, namely their promotion through targeted tourism coach packages which can be applied to Old Bazaar in Korça.

Finally, it is very important to emphasize that Old Bazaar in Korça is not simply a shopping mall but a fusion of diverse experiences based on local identity. With that said, the Bazaar should develop as a focal point where market, gastronomic area, cultural quarter, open area museum, and innovative hub perpetually intertwine.

The biggest challenge will be to create innovative tourist offers through the appropriation of traditional Bazaar practices that will allow synergy of heritage, entrepreneurship, creativity, and knowledge so that the local community can equally enjoy them.

References

Adams, C. (2007). Urban Governance and the Control of Infrastructure. *Public Works Management & Policy, 11*(3), 164–176. doi:10.1177/1087724X06297318

Albers Mohrman, S., & Lawler III, E. (2014). Designing Organizations for Sustainable Effectiveness: A New Paradigm for Organizations and Academic Researchers. *Journal of Organizational Effectiveness, 1*(1), 14–34. doi:10.1108/JOEPP-01-2014-0007

Argyris, C., & Schön, D. (1978). *Organizational Learning: A Theory of Action Approach*. Reading, MA: Addision Wesley.

Armbruster, H. et al. (2008). Organizational Innovation: The Challenge of Measuring Non-Technical Innovation in Large-Scale Surveys. *Technovation, 28*(10), 644–657.

Bashkia Korçë & DRKK Korçë. (2014). Restaurimi i Objekteve të Pazarit të Korçës.

Beavon, K. S. O. (2004). *Johannesburg: The Making and Shaping of the City*. University of South Africa, UNISA Press.

Berry, A. J., Sweeting, R., & Goto, J. (2006). The Effect of Business Advisers on the Performance of SMEs. *Journal of Small Business and Enterprise Development, 13*(1), 33–47. doi:10.1108/14626000610645298

Berry, J., Godfrey, A., McGreal, S., & Adair, A. (2010). Business Improvement Districts in Great Britain: Governance, Finance and Stakeholder Engagement. *Journal of Town & City Management, 1*(2), 128–147.

Bose, S., Roy, S. K., & Tiwari, A. K. (2016). Measuring Customer-Based Place Brand Equity (CBPBE): An Investment Attractiveness Perspective. *Journal of Strategic Marketing, 24*(7), 617–634. doi:10.1080/0965254X.2016.1148766

Briffault, R. (1999). A Government for Our Time—Business Improvement Districts and Urban Governance. Columbia Law Review, 99, 365.

Calabrese, S., Epple, D., & Romano, R. (2007). On the Political Economy of Zoning. *Journal of Public Economics, 91*(1–2), 25–49. doi:10.1016/J.JPUBECO.2006.09.004

Caruso, G., & Weber, R. (2008). Getting the Max for the Tax: An Examination of BID Performance Measures. In G. Morçöl, L. Hoyt, J. W. Meek, &

U. Zimmermann (Eds.), *Business Improvement Districts: Research, Theories, and Controversies.* New York: Routledge. doi:10.4324/9781315096025

Černe, M., Kaše, R., & Škerlavaj, M. (2016). Non-Technological Innovation Research: Evaluating the Intellectual Structure and Prospects of an Emerging Field. *Scandinavian Journal of Management, 32*(2), 69–85.

Chourabi, H., Nam, T., Walker, S., Gil-Garcia, J. R., Mellouli, S., Nahon, K., … Scholl, H. J. (2012). Understanding Smart Cities: An Integrative Framework. *2012 45th Hawaii International Conference on System Sciences* (pp. 2289–2297). IEEE. doi:10.1109/HICSS.2012.615

City Improvement District Forum. (2016). *A Quantitative and Qualitative Impact Assessment.* Johannesburg: Johannesburg CID Forum.

Comunian, R. (2011). Rethinking the Creative City. *Urban Studies, 48*(6), 1157–1179. doi:10.1177/0042098010370626

Cook, I. R. (2008). Mobilising Urban Policies: The Policy Transfer of US Business Improvement Districts to England and Wales. *Urban Studies, 45*(4), 773–795. doi:10.1177/0042098007088468

Cook, I. R. (2009). Private Sector Involvement in Urban Governance: The Case of Business Improvement Districts and Town Centre Management partnerships in England. *Geoforum, 40*(5), 930–940. doi:10.1016/J.GEOFORUM.2009.07.003

Cooke, P., & Wills, D. (1999). Small Firms, Social Capital and the Enhancement of Business Performance through Innovation Programmes. *Small Business Economics, 13*(3), 219–234. doi:10.1023/A:1008178808631

Crivello, S. (2015). Urban Policy Mobilities: The Case of Turin as a Smart City. *European Planning Studies, 23*(5), 909–921. doi:10.1080/09654313.2014.891568

Crossan, M. M., & Apaydin, M. (2010). A Multi-Dimensional Framework of Organizational Innovation: A Systematic Review of the Literature. *Journal of Management Studies, 47*(6), 1154–1191.

Daft, R. L. (1978). A Dual-Core Model of Organizational Innovation. *The Academy of Management Journal, 21*(2), 193–210.

Damanpour, F. (1991). Organizational Innovation: A Meta-Analysis of Effects of Determinants and Moderators. *The Academy of Management Journal, 34*(3), 555–590.

Damanpour, F., & Aravind, D. (2011). Managerial Innovation: Conceptions, Processes, and Antecedents. *Management and Organization Review, 8*(2), 423–454.

Damanpour, F., & Evan, W. M. (1984). Organizational Innovation and Performance: The Problem of "Organizational Lag." *Administrative Science Quarterly, 29*(3), 392–409.

Damanpour, F., Sanchez-Henriquez, F., & Chiu, H. H. (2018). Internal and External Sources and the Adoption of Innovations in Organizations. *British Journal of Management, 29*(4), 712–730.

Dassler, T., & Parker, D. (2004). Harmony or Disharmony in the Regulation and the Promotion of Competition in EU Telecommunications? A Survey of the Regulatory Offices. *Utilities Policy, 12*(1), 9–28. doi:10.1016/J.JUP.2003.08.002

Davies, M. S. (1997). Business Improvement Districts. *Washington University Journal of Urban & Contemporary Law, 52*, 187.

Devereaux Jennings, P., & Zandbergen, P. A. (1995). Ecologically Sustainable Organizations: An Institutional Approach. *Academy of Management Review, 20*(4), 1015–1052.

Didier, S., Morange, M., & Peyroux, E. (2013). The Adaptative Nature of Neoliberalism at the Local Scale: Fifteen Years of City Improvement Districts in Cape Town and Johannesburg. *Antipode, 45*(1), 121–139.

Dobson, S., & Jorgensen, A. (2014). Increasing the Resilience and Adaptive Capacity of Cities through Entrepreneurial Urbanism. *International Journal of Globalisation and Small Business, 6*(3/4), 149. doi:10.1504/IJGSB.2014.067508

Dolowitz, D. P., & Marsh, D. (2000). Learning from Abroad: The Role of Policy Transfer in Contemporary Policy-Making. *Governance, 13*(1), 5–23. doi:10.1111/0952-1895.00121

Donaldson, L. (1996). *For Positivist Organization Theory*. London: Sage Publication Ltd.. doi:10.4135/9781446280331.

Donaldson, L. (2001). *The Contingency Theory of Organizations*. London: Sage Publication Ltd. doi: 10.4135/9781452229249

Drescher, D. (2016). *Transforming Communities through Main Street: Annual Letter to Main Street Stakeholders*. Austin, TX: Texas Historical Commission.

Drescher, D. (2018). *Main Street Matters: Year 2017 in Review*. Austin, TX: Texas Historical Commission, Texas.

Driffield, N. (2001). The Impact on Domestic Productivity of Inward Investment in the UK. *The Manchester School, 69*(1), 103–119. doi:10.1111/1467-9957.00237

Farahani, L., & Lozanovska, M. (2014). A Framework for Exploring the Sense of Community and Social Life in Residential Environments. *International Journal of Architectural Research: ArchNet-IJAR, 8*(3), 223. doi:10.26687/archnet-ijar.v8i3.412

Fischel, W. A. (2004). An Economic History of Zoning and a Cure for its Exclusionary Effects. *Urban Studies, 41*(2), 317–340. doi:10.1080/0042098032000165271

Forrer, J., Kee, J. E., Newcomer, K. E., & Boyer, E. (2010). Public-Private Partnerships and the Public Accountability Question. *Public Administration Review, 70*(3), 475–484. doi:10.1111/j.1540-6210.2010.02161.x

Gartner, W. C., & Ruzzier, M. K. (2011). Tourism Destination Brand Equity Dimensions. *Journal of Travel Research, 50*(5), 471–481. doi:10.1177/0047287510379157

Geddes, M. (2006). Partnership and the Limits to Local Governance in England: Institutionalist Analysis and Neoliberalism. *International Journal of Urban and Regional Research, 30*(1), 76–97. doi:10.1111/j.1468-2427.2006.00645.x

Geuting, E. (2007). Proprietary Governance and Property Development: Using Changes in the Property-Rights Regime as a Market-Based Policy Tool. *Town Planning Review, 78*(1), 23–39. doi:10.3828/tpr.78.1.3

Gibbons, P. T., & O'Connor, T. (2005). Influences on Strategic Planning Processes among Irish SMEs*. *Journal of Small Business Management, 43*(2), 170–186. doi:10.1111/j.1540-627x.2005.00132.x

Giffinger, R., Fertner, C., Kramar, H., & Meijers, E. (2007). City-ranking of European Medium-sized Cities. *Centre of Regional Science Vienna University of Technology*, 1–12.

Giraud-Labalte, C., Pugh, K., Quaedvlieg-Mihailović, S., Sanetra-Szeliga, J., Smith, B., Vandesande, A., & Thys, C. (2015). Cultural Heritage Counts for Europe. Krakow: Cultural Heritage Counts for Europe Consortium by the International Cultural Centre (dostupno na: http://blogs. encatc. org/ culturalheritagecountsforeurope/outcomes/).

Godfrey, A. N., & Gretzel, U. (2016). The use of modern architecture in city marketing. Travel and Research Association: Advancing Tourism Research Globally. 33. Retrieved from http://scholarworks.umass.edu/ttra/2010/ Visual/33

Godin, B. (2008). Project on the Intellectual History of Innovation. INRS. Consulté à l'adresse http://www. chairefernanddumont. ucs. inrs. ca/wpcontent/ uploads/2013/11/GodinB_2009_Innovation_the_History_of_a_Category_ Workin g_Paper_No_1. pdf.

Government of Ontario. (2010). *Business Improvement Area Handbook.*

Graham, B. (2002). Heritage as Knowledge: Capital or Culture? *Urban Studies, 39*(5–6), 1003–1017. doi:10.1080/00420980220128426

Granger, R. (2010). What Now for Urban Regeneration? *Proceedings of the ICE – Urban Design and Planning, 163*(1), 9–16. doi:10.1680/udap.2010.163.1.9

Gross, J. S. (2013). Business Improvement Districts in New York: The Private Sector in Public Service or the Public Sector Privatized? *Urban Research & Practice, 6*(3), 346–364. doi:10.1080/17535069.2013.846003

Grossman, S. A. (2008). The Case of Business Improvement Districts: Special District Public—Private Cooperation in Community Revitalization. *Public Performance & Management Review, 32*(2), 290–308. doi:10.2753/ PMR1530-9576320206

Grossman, S. A. (2010). Reconceptualizing the Public Management and Performance of Business Improvement Districts. *Public Performance & Management Review, 33*(3), 361–394. doi:10.2753/PMR1530-9576330304

Hall, B. H., Lotti, F., & Mairesse, J. (2009). Innovation and Productivity in SMEs: Empirical Evidence for Italy. *Small Business Economics, 33*(1), 13–33. doi:10.1007/s11187-009-9184-8

Harrison, C., Eckman, B., Hamilton, R., Hartswick, P., Kalagnanam, J., Paraszczak, J., & Williams, P. (2010). Foundations for Smarter Cities. *IBM Journal of Research and Development, 54*(4), 1–16. doi:10.1147/JRD.2010.2048257

Hart, T., & Johnston, I. (2000). Employment, Education and Training. In *Urban Regeneration*: A Handbook Eds P Roberts, H Sykes (Sage, London) pp. 129.

Harvey, D. (1989). From Managerialism to Entrepreneurialism: The Transformation in Urban Governance in Late Capitalism. *Geografiska Annaler: Series B, Human Geography, 71*(1), 3–17. doi:10.1080/04353684.1989.11879583

Hastings, A. (1996). Unravelling the Process of "Partnership" in Urban Regeneration Policy. *Urban Studies, 33*(2), 253–268. doi:10.1080/00420989650011997

Hatry, H. (1999). Introduction. *Public Administration Review, 59*(2), 101. doi:10.2307/977629

Hefetz, A., & Warner, M. (2004). Privatization and Its Reverse: Explaining the Dynamics of the Government Contracting Process. *Journal of Public Administration Research and Theory, 14*(2), 171–190. doi:10.1093/jopart/muh012

Hochleutner, B. R. (2003). BIDs Fare Well: The Democratic Accountability of Business Improvement Districts. *New York University Law Review, 78*, 374.

Hogg, S., Medway, D., & Warnaby, G. (2003). Business Improvement Districts: An Opportunity for SME Retailing. *International Journal of Retail & Distribution Management, 31*(9), 466–469. doi:10.1108/09590550310491432

Hogg, S., Medway, D., & Warnaby, G. (2004). Town Centre Management Schemes in the UK: Marketing and Performance Indicators. *International Journal of Nonprofit and Voluntary Sector Marketing, 9*(4), 309–319. doi:10.1002/nvsm.256

Houston Jr., L. O. (1997). Business Improvement Districts: Self-Help Downtown, (June), Taylor & Francis, publisher of Local Economy, 1–16.

Hoyt, L. (2005a). Co-Ordinating Neighbourhoods-Who Should Plan? Oxford: Blackwell Publishing.

Hoyt, L. (2005b). *The business improvement district: an internationally diffused approach to revitalization.* Washington, D.C.: International Downtown Association.

Hoyt, L. (2008). From North America to Africa: The BID Model and the Role of Policy Entrepreneurs. Public Administration and Public Policy-New York, 145, 111.

Hoyt, L., & Gopal-Agge, D. (2007). The Business Improvement District Model: A Balanced Review of Contemporary Debates. *Geography Compass.* doi:10.1111/j.1749-8198.2007.00041.x

Jacobsen, B. P. (2009). Investor-Based Place Brand Equity: A Theoretical Framework. *Journal of Place Management and Development, 2*(1), 70–84. doi:10.1108/17538330910946029

Jansson, J. and D. Power (2006). *The Image of the City – Urban Branding as Constructed Capabilities in Nordic City Regions.* Oslo, Nordic Innovation Centre.

Jarrar, Y., & Schiuma, G. (2007). Measuring Performance in the Public Sector: Challenges and Trends. *Measuring Business Excellence, 11*(4), 4–8. doi:10.1108/13683040710837883

Jeffrey P, Pounder J, 2000, "Physical and Environmental Aspects", In *Urban Regeneration: A Handbook*, Eds P Roberts, H Sykes (pp. 86–108). London: Sage Publications.

Jessop, B. (2000), 'Globalisation, entrepreneurial cities, and the social economy', in P. Hamel, H. Lustiger-Thaler & M. Mayer (eds.), *Urban Movements in a Globalizing World*, 81–100. London: Routledge.

Jessop, B., & Sum, N.-L. (2000). An Entrepreneurial City in Action: Hong Kong's Emerging Strategies in and for (Inter)Urban Competition. *Urban Studies, 37*(12), 2287–2313. doi:10.1080/00420980020002814

Jonas, A. E. G., McCarthy, L. Redevelopment at All Costs? A Critical Review and Examination of the American Model of Urban Management and Regeneration. In *Urban Regeneration Management*. Ed. By Diamond, J. et al., Routledge, New York, 2010.

Jonas, A. E. G., & Wood, A. (2016). *Territory, the State, and Urban Politics: A Critical Appreciation of the Selected Writings of Kevin R. Cox*. Routledge.

Jones, P., & Evans, J. (2013). *Urban Regeneration in the UK: Boom, Bust and Recovery*. Sage.

Judd, D. (2003). Reconstructing Regional Politics: Special Purpose Authorities and Municipal Governments. A Great Cities Institute Working Paper June.

Kallamata, K. (1998). Mbi restaurimin e pazarit të Korçes. *Monumentet*, (2), 159–162.

Kavaratzis, M. (2004). From City Marketing to City Branding: Towards a Theoretical Framework for Developing City Brands. *Place Branding, 1*(1), 58–73. doi:10.1057/palgrave.pb.5990005

Kavaratzis, M. (2007). City Marketing: The Past, the Present and Some Unresolved Issues. *Geography Compass, 1*(3), 695–712. doi:10.1111/j.1749-8198.2007.00034.x

Kavaratzis, M., & Ashworth, G. J. (2005). City Branding: An Effective Assertion of Identity or a Transitory Marketing Trick? *Tijdschrift Voor Economische En Sociale Geografie, 96*(5), 506–514. doi:10.1111/j.1467-9663.2005.00482.x

Keupp, M. M., Palmié, M., & Gassmann, O. (2012). The Strategic Management of Innovation: A Systematic Review and Paths for Future Research. *International Journal of Management Reviews, 14*(4), 367–390.

Laforet, S. (2011). A Framework of Organisational Innovation and Outcomes in SMEs. *International Journal of Entrepreneurial Behavior & Research, 17*(4), 380–408. doi:10.1108/13552551111139638

Lam, A. (2004). Organizational Innovation. In J. Fagerberg, D. Mowery, & R. Nelson (Eds.), *The Oxford Handbook of Innovation*. Oxford: Oxford University Press2004. doi:10.1007/978-1-4020-6071-7_5

Landow, P., & Ebdon, C. (2012). Public-Private Partnerships, Public Authorities, and Democratic Governance. *Public Performance & Management Review, 35*(4), 727–752. doi:10.2753/PMR1530-9576350408

Languillon-Aussel, R. (2014). The Burst Bubble and the Privatisation of Planning in Tokyo. Metropolitiques. Available (consulted 8 June 2014) at: http://www. metropolitiques. eu/The-burst-bubble-and-the. html.

Lehtonen, M., 2015. Indicators: tools for informing, monitoring or controlling? In: Jordan, A.J., Turnpenny, J.R. (Eds.), *The Tools of Policy Formulation. Actors, Capacities, Venues and Effects*. Elgaronline, pp. 76–99.

Lemus-Aguilar, I., & Hidalgo, A. (2016). The Design of a Sustainable Organization: A Solid Path through Innovation. *INGENIO Days 2016: Eu-SPRI Forum Early Career Researcher Conference (ECC): "Science, Innovation and the University: Keys to Social Impact,"* 1–15.

Lin, N. (1999). Building a Network Theory of Social Capital. *Connections, 22*(1), 28–51. doi:10.4324/9781315129457-1

Liouris, C., & Deffner, A. (2005). City Marketing-a Significant Planning Tool for Urban Development in a Globalised Economy. 45th Congress of the European Regional Science Association, ERSA conference papers.

Lepore, J. (2014). The Disruption Machine. *The New Yorker, 23*, 30–36.

Lloyd, M. G., McCarthy, J., McGreal, S., & Berry, J. (2003). Business Improvement Districts, Planning and Urban Regeneration. *International Planning Studies, 8*(4), 295–321. doi:10.1080/1356347032000153133

Longoni, A., Golini, R., & Cagliano, R. (2014). The Role of New Forms of Work Organization in Developing Sustainability Strategies in Operations. *International Journal of Production Economics, 147*(PART A), 147–160. doi:10.1016/j.ijpe.2013.09.009

MacDonald, H. (1996). Why Business Improvement Districts Work. *Civic Bulletin, 4*, 1–3.

Mair, J. (2012). A Review of Business Events Literature. *Event Management, 16*(2), 133–141. doi:10.3727/152599512X13343565268339

Malecki, E. (2004). Jockeying for Position: What It Means and Why It Matters to Regional Development Policy When Places Compete. *Regional Studies, 38*(9), 1101–1120. doi:10.1080/0034340042000292665

Marriott, N., & Marriott, P. (2000). Professional Accountants and the Development of a Management Accounting Service for the Small Firm: Barriers and Possibilities. *Management Accounting Research, 11*(4), 475–492. doi:10.1006/MARE.2000.0142

McCann, E., & Ward, K. (2010). Relationality/Territoriality: Toward a Conceptualization of Cities in the World. *Geoforum, 41*(2), 175–184. doi:10.1016/J.GEOFORUM.2009.06.006

McCarthy, J. (2007). *Partnership, Collaborative Planning and Urban Regeneration.* Routledge. doi:10.4324/9781315599588

Michel, B., & Stein, C. (2015). Reclaiming the European City and Lobbying for Privilege. *Urban Affairs Review, 51*(1), 74–98. doi:10.1177/1078087414522391

Miles, I. (2005). Knowledge Intensive Business Services: Prospects and Policies. *Foresight, 7*(6), 39–63.

Miles, S., & Paddison, R. (2005). Introduction: The Rise and Rise of Culture-led Urban Regeneration. *Urban Studies, 42*(5–6), 833–839. doi:10.1080/00420980500107508

Mintzberg, H. (1979). *The Structuring of Organizations.* Englewood Cliffs, NJ: Prentice Hall.

Mitchell, J. (1999). Business Improvement Districts and Innovative Service Delivery. New York. doi:10.1111/j.1360-0443.1991.tb01699.x

Mitchell, J. (2001). Business Improvement Districts and the Management of Innovation. *The American Review of Public Administration, 31*(2), 201–217.

Mitchell, J. (2008). *Business Improvement Districts and the Shape of American Cities.* Albany: State University of New York Press.

Mitsubishi Estate Co. (2016). *Annual Report 2015: Enhancing the Possibilities of Tomorrow.* Otemachi Building, 6–1, Otemachi 1-chome, Chiyoda-ku, Tokyo 100-8133, Japan. Available at http://www.mec.co.jp/index_e.html

Miyazawa, M. (2006). Downtown Revitalization in Japan: Examination of the Town Management Organization Model (Doctoral dissertation, Massachusetts Institute of Technology).

Morçöl, G., Vasavada, T., & Kim, S. (2014). Business Improvement Districts in Urban Governance. *Administration & Society, 46*(7), 796–824. doi:10.1177/0095399712473985

Morçöl, G., & Wolf, J. F. (2010). Understanding Business Improvement Districts: A New Governance Framework. *Public Administration Review, 70*(6), 906–913. doi:10.1111/j.1540-6210.2010.02222.x

Morçöl, G., & Zimmermann, U. (2006). Metropolitan Governance and Business Improvement Districts. *International Journal of Public Administration, 29*(1–3), 5–29. doi:10.1080/01900690500408965

Morcol, G., Hoyt, L., Meek, J. W., & Zimmermann, U. (Eds.). (2017). *Business Improvement Districts: Research, Theories, and Controversies.* Routledge.

Mossberger, K., & Wolman, H. (2003). Policy Transfer as a Form of Prospective Policy Evaluation: Challenges and Recommendations. *Public Administration Review, 63*(4), 428–440. doi:10.1111/1540-6210.00306

Needham, B., & Louw, E. (2006). Institutional Economics and Policies for Changing Land Markets: The Case of Industrial Estates in the Netherlands. *Journal of Property Research, 23*(1), 75–90. doi:10.1080/09599910600748675

Nieto, M. J., & Santamaria, L. (2010). Technological Collaboration: Bridging the Innovation Gap between Small and Large Firms*. *Journal of Small Business Management, 48*(1), 44–69. doi:10.1111/j.1540-627X.2009.00286.x

Nonaka, I. (1994). A dynamic theory of organizational knowledge creation. *Organization science, 5*(1), 14–37.

Nonaka, I., & Takeuchi, H. (1995). *The Knowledge-creating Company: How Japanese Companies Create the Dynamics of Innovation*, Oxford University Press, New York.

Noon, D., J. Smith-Canham ve M. Eagland (2000) Economic regeneration and funding. Peter Roberts ve Hugh Sykes (der.). *Urban Regeneration.* London, Thousand Oaks, New Delhi: Sage Publications. 61–85.

Nowotny, Helga, ed. 2006. *Cultures of Technology and the Quest for Innovation.* New York: Berghahn Books.

O'Dwyer, M., Gilmore, A., & Carson, D. (2009). Innovative Marketing in SMEs. *European Journal of Marketing, 43*(1/2), 46–61. doi:10.1108/03090560910923238

O'Sullivan, A. (2012). *Urban Economics,* 8th Edition. Boston, MA: McGraw-Hill/Irwin.

Paddison, R. (1993). City Marketing, Image Reconstruction and Urban Regeneration. *Urban Studies, 30*(2), 339–349. doi:10.1080/00420989320080331

Papadopoulos, N. (2004). Place Branding: Evolution, Meaning and Implications. *Place Branding, 1*(1), 36–49. doi:10.1057/palgrave.pb.5990003

Patwardhan, A. M., Ford, J. B., & Clarke, G. R. G. (2018). The Neo-Weberian Contingency Theory of Innovation. *Journal of Management and Marketing Research, 21*, 1–31.

Peel, D., & Lloyd, M. G. (2005a). Development Plans, Lesson-Drawing and Model Policies in Scotland. *International Planning Studies, 10*(3–4), 265–287. doi:10.1080/13563470500378853

Peel, D., & Lloyd, M. G. (2005b). A Case for Business Improvement Districts in Scotland: Policy Transfer in Practice? *Planning Practice and Research, 20*(1), 89–95. doi:10.1080/02697450500261780

Peel, D., Lloyd, M. G., & Lord, A. (2009). Business Improvement Districts and the Discourse of Contractualism. *European Planning Studies, 17*(3), 401–422. doi:10.1080/09654310802618044

Peyroux, E. (2006). City Improvement Districts in Johannesburg: Assessing the Political and Socio-spatial Implications of Private-led Urban Regeneraion. TRIALOG, 9–14.

Peyroux, E. (2008). City Improvement Districts in Johannesburg. An Examination of the Local Variations of the BID Model. In R. Pu¨tz (Hg.), Passau: Business Improvement Districts, pp. 139–162.

Peyroux, E., Pütz, R., & Glasze, G. (2012). Business Improvement Districts (BIDs): Internationalisation and Contextualisation of a "Travelling Concept." *European Urban and Regional Studies, 19*(2), 111–120.

Pierre, J. (1998). *Partnerships in Urban Governance: European and American Experience*. London: Macmillan Press.

Poister, T. H. (2008). *Measuring Performance in Public and Nonprofit Organizations*, Jossey – Bass, San Francisco, CA.

Ponzini, D., & Rossi, U. (2010). Becoming a Creative City: The Entrepreneurial Mayor, Network Politics and the Promise of an Urban Renaissance. *Urban Studies, 47*(5), 1037–1057. doi:10.1177/0042098009353073

Quinn, B., McKitterick, L., McAdam, R., & Brennan, M. (2013). Innovation in Small-Scale Retailing. *The International Journal of Entrepreneurship and Innovation, 14*(2), 81–93. doi:10.5367/ijei.2013.0111

Riza, E. (1978). Ansamblet ndërtimore të pazareve dhe restaurimi i tyre. (Les ensembles de marchés et leur restauration). *Monumentet Tirana, 15*, 117–138.

Roberts, P. (2008). The Evolution, Definition and Purpose of Urban Regeneration. In *Urban Regeneration: A Handbook* (pp. 9–36). 1 Oliver's Yard, 55 City Road, London EC1Y 1SP United Kingdom: SAGE Publications Ltd. doi:10.4135/9781446219980.n2

Robertson, K. A. (2004). The Main Street Approach to Downtown Development: An Examination of the Four-Point Program. *Journal of Architectural and Planning Research*. Locke Science Publishing Company, Inc. doi:10.2307/43031059

Rothrock, L. L. A. (2008). Business Improvement Districts: An Effective Revitalization Tool for Massachusetts' Forgotten Cities? (Doctoral dissertation, Massachusetts Institute of Technology).

Ryberg-Webster, S., & Kinahan, K. L. (2014). Historic Preservation and Urban Revitalization in the Twenty-first Century. doi:10.1177/0885412213510524

Sager, T. (2011). Neo-Liberal Urban Planning Policies: A Literature Survey 1990–2010. *Progress in Planning, 76*(4), 147–199. doi:10.1016/J.PROGRESS. 2011.09.001

Sarmento, M., Farhangmehr, M., & Simões, C. (2015). Participating in Business-to-Business Trade Fairs: Does the Buying Function Matter? *Journal of Convention & Event Tourism, 16*(4), 273–297. doi:10.1080/15470148.20 15.1043608

Schwab, A., Taylor, L., Wilson, J., Griffiths, J., Masundire, C., & Rich, H. (2016). *The evolution of London's Business Improvement Districts.* Retrieved from Greater London Authority: https://www.london.gov.uk/sites/default/ files/evolution_of_londons_bids_march2016_web_0 20316.pdf

Smitha, K. C. (2017). Entrepreneurial Urbanism in India: A Framework. In *Entrepreneurial Urbanism in India* (pp. 1–31). Singapore: Springer Singapore. doi:10.1007/978-981-10-2236-4_1

Stahl, K. A. (2013). Neighborhood Empowerment and the Future of the City. *University of Pennsylvania Law Review, 161*(4), 939–1008. doi:10.2139/ ssrn.1870337

Stokes, R. J. (2006). Business Improvement Districts and Inner City Revitalization: The Case of Philadelphia's Frankford Special Services District. *International Journal of Public Administration, 29*(1–3), 173–186. doi:10.1080/01900690500409021

Stokes, R. J. (2007). Business Improvement Districts and Small Business Advocacy: The Case of San Diego's Citywide BID Program. *Economic Development Quarterly, 21*(3), 278–291. doi:10.1177/0891242407302325

Sullivan, A., Huang, C.-S., & Abrams, R. F. (2006). Assessing the Economic Revitalization Impact of Urban Design Improvements: The Texas Main Street Program.

Symes, M., & Steel, M. (2003). Lessons from America: The Role of Business Improvement Districts as an Agent of Urban Regeneration. *Town Planning Review, 74*(3), 301–313. doi:10.3828/tpr.74.3.3

Tallon, A. (2013). *Urban Regeneration in the UK.* Routledge. doi:10.4324/ 9780203802847

Tasci, A. D. A., & Gartner, W. C. (2007). Destination Image and Its Functional Relationships. *Journal of Travel Research, 45*(4), 413–425. doi:10.1177/ 0047287507299569

The Ontario BIAs Association, O. (2017). *Return on Investment of BIAs Report.*

Thëllimi, N., & Larti, I. (2008). *My Birthplace: Korca and Devolli.* Tiranë: Shtëpia Botuese "Erik."

Trebeck, K. (2007). *Private Sector Contribution to Regeneration: Concepts, Actions and Synergies.* Centre for Public Policy for Regions, University of Glasgow.

Unger, A. (2016). *Business Improvement Districts in the United States: Private Government and Public Consequences.* Cham, Switzerland: Springer International Publishing AG.

Walburn, D. (2005). Trends in Entrepreneurship Policy. *Local Economy, 20*(1), 90–92. doi:10.1080/0269094042000326652

Wang, C., Walker, E., & Redmond, J. (2007). Explaining the Lack of Strategic Planning in SMEs: The Importance of Owner Motivation. *International Journal of Organizational Behavior, 12*(121), 1–16.

Ward, K. (2006). "Policies in Motion", Urban Management and State Restructuring: The Trans-Local Expansion of Business Improvement Districts. *International Journal of Urban and Regional Research, 30*(1), 54–75. doi:10.1111/j.1468-2427.2006.00643.x

Ward, K. (2007). Business Improvement Districts: Policy Origins, Mobile Policies and Urban Liveability. *Geography Compass, 1*(3), 657–672. doi:10.1111/j.1749-8198.2007.00022.x

Ward, K. (2010). Entrepreneurial Urbanism and Business Improvement Districts in the State of Wisconsin: A Cosmopolitan Critique. *Annals of the Association of American Geographers, 100*(5), 1177–1196. doi:10.1080/00045608.2010.520211

Ward, K. (2012). Entrepreneurial Urbanism, Policy Tourism, and the Making Mobile of Policies. In *The New Blackwell Companion to the City* (pp. 726–737). Oxford: Wiley-Blackwell. doi:10.1002/9781444395105.ch63

Ward, K., & Cook, I. R. (2014). Business Improvement Districts in the UK: Territorialising a 'Global'Model? (Vol. 13). Imagining Urban Futures Working Paper.

Warner, M. E., & Hefetz, A. (2008). Managing Markets for Public Service: The Role of Mixed Public–private Delivery of City Services. *Public Administration Review, 68*(1), 155–166.

Zenker, S., & Braun, E. (2010, June). The Place Brand Centre–A Conceptual Approach for the Brand Management of Places. In 39th European Marketing Academy Conference, Copenhagen, Denmark (pp. 1–8).

Index

Printed in the United States
by Baker & Taylor Publisher Services